RISKING

CRAZY

DENY SELF
FOLLOW JESUS

JASON TAYLOR

randall house

13-ISBN 9780892656561

Dedicated to those who have walked the *Risking Crazy* life with me: my wife Melissa, my two kids, Hudson and Haley, the wonderful staff, volunteers, and people of The Vertical Church. I also dedicate this work to my parents who instilled in me the truth that I can do anything God wants me to do.

Table of Contents

INTRODUCTION

Beginning at a young age, Jesus tugged at my heart for those who were less fortunate than I was. He called me to move beyond my comfort and touch lives in such a way that some might call me crazy.

Risking Crazy is all about listening to the Holy Spirit and obeying His voice by taking calculated risks—that some might call crazy—for His glory.

I still remember the day my dad woke me up and told me we were going to pick up a couple of boys from a poverty-stricken part of my town. In my mind, I never thought we were rich. I knew plenty of people who had more than we did. After I met these two boys, I realized that I had much indeed, and I was very fortunate to even have a roof over my head. This was definitely out of my comfort zone. My dad broke through that and had in his heart to reach out to these young boys.

That day my dad decided to "Risk Crazy." This left an impression on me forever etched into my mind. On that day, we did things that were a normal part of my life. We went to the Stockyards (a place where cattle and other livestock are auctioned and sold), rode our mini bike (which I did almost every day and did not think twice about it), and even got a Happy Meal at McDonalds. These were normal things in my life, but for these two young boys, this was a special day.

I do not remember their names, and they probably do not remember mine, but I do remember the joy that was in their eyes after spending the day with my family. But beyond that, Jesus put a call in my heart, compassion, a tear in my eye for the hurting, helpless, and the poor around me.

Since that day, I have been on a journey to lead a life of kindness and compassion with the message of Jesus as well as lead others to do the same.

As a lead pastor now in my mid-thirties, God has given me the privilege to start a church based on these core values.

This book is a call to those who identify themselves as Christ followers to live beyond your fears, status quo, and "stuff" that you have accumulated. This is a call to Christians to realize there are people in your communities, cities, and towns who are praying to God and crying out to Him for help.

It is time we wake up and hear the call of God to be the hands and feet of Jesus. It is time we live a life that involves "Risking Crazy" every day of our lives. Knowing that we will never arrive, nor be perfect in our attitudes and actions, but Jesus has called us to show His love in practical ways to people we pass every day.

My prayer is that by the end of this book you will continue to take risky steps of faith for Jesus!

CHAPTER 1

Are You Going to Do This or Not?

As we look at the world around us, we see greater needs than we have ever seen. At times, it is a bit overwhelming.

For the person who has put his life in Jesus' hands, our individual communities seem to be getting worse. The words of Jesus to "Go and make disciples," (Matthew 28:19) ring in our ears and hearts, but, at times, we feel like our efforts are not making a difference.

When we first started The Vertical Church in Yuma, Arizona, it was a really slow go. But saying yes to the small promptings of Jesus to "deny [yourself] and take up [your] cross daily and follow me" (Luke 9:23) has led to people's lives being changed all over Yuma. Obeying these "little" promptings led us to live a lifestyle of risking crazy—taking risks—that some might call crazy—for Jesus.

Of course, the poor, needy, and helpless in our city are not all served, not all of Yuma has started following Jesus. But we are starting to make a dent.

For me, it all started with a small prompting by the Holy Spirit to become a preacher of the gospel.

I grew up in a Christian home that sat on 2603 Roseville Road in Glasgow, Kentucky. From a small child, my parents inspired me to do whatever I set my mind to do.

But God's call to become a preacher was different from my parents' encouragement because it was not what I really wanted to do. God stirred my soul as a 13-year-old boy to lay aside any dream I had, to follow Him, and take steps of faith for the rest of my life.

Finally, at the age of 15, on a fall evening, we drove to a revival at our church. I do not remember the message at all. I sat on the third pew in that church and knew from the first song that I was going to stand up and tell the entire church: "God had called me to preach!"

The butterflies grew in my stomach as the service pro-gressed: one song, then three songs, offering was taken, next a special song was performed, and then the preacher presented his sermon. At the end of the service, when the time came for "testimonies," I stood up with every ounce of faith, confidence, and puberty-stricken voice I had and said with authority: "God has called me to preach, and I have said yes!"

At that moment, my life changed forever. At that moment, I answered the question: Are you going to do this or not? It changed my whole trajectory in life and set me on a path of lis-tening and obeying the Spirit's voice when He called.

YOU MUST START SOMEWHERE

The lifestyle of taking risks must start with the Holy Spirit calling you and speaking to your soul. Here is the truth: He is calling you! You do not have to wait for an audible voice, light-ning bolt, or imaginary writing on a wall. The Bible has already given us commands:

"But you will receive power when the Holy Spirit comes on you; and you will be my witnesses in Jerusalem, and in all Judea and Samaria, and to the ends of the earth" (Acts 1:8).

"Again Jesus said, 'Peace be with you! As the Father has sent me, I am sending you'" (John 20:21).

"Therefore go and make disciples of all nations" (Matthew 28:19).

I could go on and on, but these are some of the famous verses from the Bible. The fact is that God is calling you to "risk crazy" with your life. He is calling you to take calculated risks for Him that some may call crazy. The question is: Are you going to do this or not?

God may not be calling you to be a preacher, pastor, or missionary. But one thing I know, God is calling you to take steps of trusting Him in your daily life.

IT STARTS BY SAYING "YES"

God has spoken to us by His Word, but He is also prompting us in our everyday lives to take faith risks.

As a 15-year-old boy, I did not have that much to give up. What was in my heart was just a dream. The dream was not all that great. Up to that time, I wanted to be a doctor, NBA star, or a NFL star. I finally realized that I had neither the skill nor brains for those. I had determined I could just be a sports medicine trainer. So for me at that age, there was not much to give up.

But then again, being uncomfortable is something to give up. Going to college, getting a degree, and getting a good paying job was comfortable for me. The truth is that is what was expected of me, in my mind. Everyone is different. However,

3

everyone has some level of comfort that they have to give up in order to follow Jesus wherever He leads.

Do not lose hope. It is in this moment that Jesus really wants to use you. The moment that you realize you cannot do what He is asking is the exact moment the Holy Spirit can empower you and equip you to do what He is asking. This is the starting place. This is the moment you give up on your self and start saying, "Yes!".

I am not talking about selling everything you own and moving to a third world country to take the gospel to an unreached people group (although God may be calling some of you to do that). I am talking about starting by saying, "Yes!"

Are you going to do this or not?

I SURRENDER ALL

Surrender is the first step. You must come to a place in your life where you realize all the material things you have accumulated will not last for eternity...the things you strive for are not the best God has for you. Before you can say yes to the other things, you have to surrender to God. This is no small task. Deep inside of you, everything is crying out to do things your own way and not God's. The culture around us is prodding us to get more, gain more, and be more on our own and for our self. But God is calling us to surrender. Jesus inside of you is asking you to throw your hands up and say, "I'm done with my self, I want to want what you want, Oh God!"

What do you need to surrender?

Comfort: The very thing that God may be asking you to do will probably be out of your comfort zone. Risking Crazy is about living out of our comfort zone.

Selfishness: As a Christ follower, this is a daily battle.

Life: This includes everything you are. Remember what Jesus said was the greatest commandments? Mark 12:30-31 tells us, "Love the Lord your God with all your heart and with all your soul and with all your mind and with all your strength. The second is this: 'Love your neighbor as yourself.'"

None of the above can be done without grace showing up in your life first. Jesus showed you grace at the moment you believed on Him for salvation. Nevertheless, grace does not end there. Grace is a daily outpouring that happens through the power and person of the Holy Spirit in our life causing us to be able to surrender. This grace gives us the power to love God, and love others. We serve and work and surrender because of grace, not to receive more grace. That "Amazing Grace" is what spurs us on to be able to surrender. This grace never leaves us.

NEXT STEP

I want to challenge you right now to stop whatever you are doing. Lay aside this book, get on your face before God, pour out your heart to Him surrendering everything you are. Through His grace, you will be able to accept His will for your life. It is not a common daily occurrence for me to physically get on my knees and bow my face to the floor before God. But when I do, I usually mean business. It is beyond my comfort. Will you join me in taking a moment and praying this prayer on your knees with face bowed before God?

The Risking Crazy Prayer: Father, I come to You because of what Jesus accomplished for me through His death and resurrection. I confess to You my attitudes of selfishness, love of comfort, and greed. Please make my life—my desires, my perspectives—what You want, what You desire. I want to say yes to Your plans. Amen.

CHAPTER 2

CALCULATION

Fast-forward a few years. I graduated college, got married, and took my first full-time ministry position at a church in South Roxana, Illinois. I was the youth pastor, associate pastor, and worship pastor. I taught in the Christian high school; whatever else I was asked to do came under my job description. It was a great time of growth in my walk with Christ, ministry, and even as a young husband.

We were comfortable. We bought our first house and began planning our lives in that small town working with the youth until we retired.

Then God began to move in my heart, in the same way He did when I was younger and struggling with this "call" to be a preacher. I knew God was stirring me to do something different, but I did not really have clarity. I began to pray more. I began to seek Him as I did when I was 13.

SURRENDER IS A REPETITIVE OPTION

As a follower of Jesus, He continually calls us out of our comfort. There are times in our lives when He taps us on the shoulder and says, "I am going this way. Are you going to join Me?" At that moment, we must decide to surrender, yet once again, to the call to risk crazy for Him.

7

So just because we surrender once does not mean we will always live in a state of surrender. In fact, we all have innate desires to get all we can so we will live all of our days in our self-made comfort zone.

This is why Jesus teaches us to deny ourselves (Luke 9:23). He knew we would get complacent and not want to move when He was moving. This could be why the early Church had to experience persecution so they would be forced to scatter and spread Jesus everywhere. They had gotten comfortable and forgotten the call to go.

For Melissa and me, we had gotten comfortable doing what we had been trained to do by our predecessors and college education. However, Jesus was saying something different. I started to pray a prayer of surrender again and tell Jesus I would do whatever He asked. Then He asked...

START A CHURCH

Literally, I questioned God: "Say what? You want me to start a church?" I remember the Spirit moving inside of me and saying, "But you said anything!"

I was caught. I had to decide: Was I going to take this risk and start a church, or just be comfortable? As I explained to Melissa what I believed God was asking us to do, she was not so quick to say yes. In fact, she thought maybe we should pray a lot more. So we did.

I remember specifically asking God to move on Melissa's heart if He really wanted us to start a church.

In the meantime, we were busy with ministry, coming into our own as a young couple, and wanting to start a family. While God was calling me to start a church, we found out Melissa was pregnant. We were very excited. The whole starting a church idea kind of grew quieter, but what we didn't know was that

God was doing something spiritual inside both of us while also something physical was happening inside of Melissa. Looking back, I see how God's hand was on it all.

Sometimes when we are asked to step beyond the norm, we do not see God's hand in the moment. But, years later, we can definitely see how He had a grand plan that we could have never written on our own.

This scenario brings us back to the definition I laid out for "risking crazy": **Listening to the Holy Spirit and obeying His voice by taking *calculated* risks—that some might call crazy—for His glory.**

Notice the word *calculated*. Risking crazy is not about running headlong into the waves of the unknown. There is a thought process involved.

The first Person already planning your risk is Jesus. He has a plan in place. He knows what is going to happen.

So many times, we see what God is asking, but are afraid to jump in because we do not know the details. The fact is we will never know the details, but we can trust in the One who created the details.

Proverbs 3:5-6 reminds us, "***Trust in the LORD*** with all your heart and lean not on your own understanding; in all your ways submit to him and he will make your paths straight."

There are three commands and one promise:

- Trust in the LORD with all your heart = command. This takes us back to surrender.
- Lean not on your own understanding = command. You do not know the future. Trust that God has already calculated each step, even for you.
- In all your ways submit to him = command. Again, surrender is the issue.

- He will make your paths straight = promise. You can count on Him.

NOT ONE, BUT TWO

We were so excited that Melissa was pregnant. We really wanted to have an ultrasound and see our baby for the first time. But as it goes with insurance companies, we had to wait a certain number of weeks.

However, we had a connection to the local crisis pregnancy center that had an ultrasound machine and was more than willing to give us a free scan. As they rolled the ultrasound wand across my wife's belly, the expression on the nurse's face became perplexed. She said, "Here is your baby!" We looked on the screen and saw an outline of a baby. Then she said, "And here is your other baby!"

Yes, you read that right; we were having TWINS! My knees immediately buckled! I had to sit down.

Do not get me wrong; we were happy, but absolutely scared! Could this really be happening? I remember thinking: "God, You are calling us to start a church, and then You give us not one, but two babies? I have never had one; how do I raise two?"

On November 13, 2001, three months before their due date, the twins were born. Hudson, my son, weighed one pound, 10 ounces. Haley, my daughter, weighed one pound, 11 ounces. They were literally miracles in the palms of our hands. The days that followed were rough. It was a rollercoaster ride. Hudson had eye issues, the possibility of being blind, a hole in his heart, and breathing complications. Haley had blood transfusions as well as breathing issues. For the next two-and-a-half months, our lives were put on hold, yet God was moving in our hearts like never before.

THE GROWING OF OUR FAITH

God drove us to our knees during this time. We prayed fervently like never before for miracles to happen in the lives of our babies. They did! Hudson's hole in his heart miraculously closed! His eyes miraculously escaped possible surgery after surgery! Their breathing issues disappeared with no long-term chronic complications! We brought those babies home from the hospital two-and-a-half months later knowing God had healed them. God had also grown our faith to believe He could do anything—including start a church through us.

God had a calculated plan for their early arrival. Through their early arrival and miraculous healing, He knew He could get our attention and grow our faith to believe Him for anything. In my mind, starting a church was no big deal; God had healed my babies, and He could do anything!

Melissa started to believe this as well. God changed her heart to be willing to do whatever God was asking of us.

Sometimes in our deepest pain, we do not see what God is doing for His glory, but one day we will. In fact, you may be going through or have gone through something where the miracle did not come, healing did not break through, and someone may have even died. In moments like this, we must know that although we do not get the answer we want to our prayers, God has answered and has a different plan. Sometimes we know that plan now, but, at other times, we may never know until we stand before Him.

We can know this: "Trust in the LORD with all your heart, and lean not on your own understanding; in all your ways submit to him, and he will make your paths straight" (Proverbs 3:5-6).

SELF GETS IN THE WAY

We wake up selfish. We go to bed selfish. We live out every-day selfish. We are consumed with self.

But you do not have to fear. Through the power and person of the Holy Spirit, we can break through selfish desires. Paul wrote in Galatians that one of the fruits of the Holy Spirit is self-control: "But the fruit of the Spirit is love, joy, peace, forbear-ance, kindness, goodness, faithfulness, gentleness, and self-control" (Galatians 5:22-23).

Self-control begins with denying yourself.

The truth is that Jesus is ultimately in control of your life. As we discussed, He has a plan for your life. God is in control and you can have self-control, through the person of the Holy Spirit living in you.

This means you can make conscious choices in an unselfish or selfish way that affects you and others around you. When we are operating in self-control, we are actively choosing to make unselfish choices in everything we do.

For example, let's say that I am an alcoholic. But, I am get-ting help. I am trying to overcome this addiction. Before I invited Jesus into my life, I had no power to overcome this addiction. Now I know that through the power and person of the Holy Spir-it living in me, I can break free from the chains of addiction. So I start believing that and then my behavior changes in accor-dance to that belief. Let's say I have been sober now for a year. I have been choosing self-control and unselfishness over my self-ish desire to have that drunken "escape." The moment I choose to drink again is the moment I start falling into selfishness. It is a selfish choice:

1. I want to escape my circumstances.
2. I do not care about what my family thinks.

3. I may lose relationships.
4. I may hurt others physically and relationally because of my choice.

When we allow self to get in the way, we choose not to practice self-control; and, thus, we lead a life of selfishness.

We need a revolution of people who will wake up each day and realize that Jesus has already formed the plan and we can trust Him. God wants us to deny our self daily by not letting self get in the way. What are you doing on a daily basis to "die to self"?

NEXT STEPS

1. Determine today what selfish desire is holding you back from taking the next step that Jesus is asking you to take.
2. Meet with a spiritual mentor or friend who can hold you accountable to start denying yourself daily.
3. Ask Jesus right now to open your eyes to the needs around you. Ask Him to remove any bit of selfishness that is holding you back. As He puts that picture of selfishness in your mind, surrender it back to Jesus.
4. Challenge your family to join you on this endeavor: If you are a parent, get with your kids and spouse, asking them to pray the risking crazy prayer (page 5) for your family. As a family, consider what are some selfish desires you need to deny?

CHAPTER 3

YOUR PART

Risking crazy is all about listening to the Holy Spirit and obeying His voice by taking calculated risks—that some might call crazy—for His glory. This way of living starts with following the commands of Jesus to "deny yourself," which is a daily surrender to God's rule over and through your life. As you and I do this, Jesus will call us out of our comfort zone into a place of uncertainty. Nevertheless, we can have hope because Jesus has already planned the path before us. We can live with the assurance that He will see us through.

With that said, there comes a time in this lifetime process that we must "do our part." In the Bible, it is called obedience. We can listen to the voice of God all day long. We can even verbally in prayer surrender to what He wants. But at the end of the day, we must get up and obey what He has commanded. Jesus said it like this: "If you love me, keep my commands" (John 14:15).

It is easy to get excited about what God is asking you to do, but it is another thing to follow through with it. Reputation is at stake.

You might be thinking, "I do not care what others think about me." But the truth is most people care what others think. The reason I know we care is that our level of obedience determines whether we care.

If we truly did not care what others thought, we would obey Jesus without question. We would jump into what He is asking us to do. We would not question it, nor try to get out of it.

Denying yourself is about putting your reputation on the line. When Jesus first said, "Deny yourself," He was speaking to a crowd that was not yet following Him (Luke 9). Do not get me wrong; the disciples where there and possibly some of the crowd from the "feeding of the 5,000," Jesus had a following, but they had not yet tasted salvation nor had the Holy Spirit living in them. He was basically saying to this crowd: To be My disciple, you must not care what others think. Drop your reputation to follow Me.

But what about those who already believe Jesus is the Savior?

Denying yourself is not just an entrance into the Christian life, but it is also how we grow deeper into the gospel everyday. It is how we live out the life of Christ in our daily walk. The power of the gospel is released through our self-denial and obedience to what He is asking. But it usually is not easy.

I AM PRETTY STUBBORN AND SO ARE YOU

As our babies came home from the hospital, God started prompting me again about planting a church. So I went back to just "seeking God." Isn't it amazing how much time we put into "seeking God" about a matter when we already know the answer? But this is not necessarily time wasted.

I set aside every Monday to pray and fast. During this time, God asked me to do something crazy. He asked me to go on a 40-day fast.

Fasting on Mondays was hard enough. But 40 days straight? No way. I love food.

As I look back, I realize that God was again building my faith. In my "putting off God" season, He was building my faith.

I am so glad God does not give up on us. He just keeps pressing and building our faith.

You may feel like you are done. There is no way God would use you now because you have said "no" too many times. God does not operate that way. He has been longing for you to say "yes" and has not given up on you.

It is amazing to me how the grace of God is so boundless. There is no end to it. He continues to call and beckon you to obey His voice. Just say "yes."

After much prayer, I finally said, "yes" to the 40-day fast. As I completed the 40 days, I realized why God had called me to it. The miracle in the fast was not just that God helped me go without solid food for those 40 days. In my mind, that seemed impossible. After completion of the fast, it was as if God said to me, "Jason, I took care of your kids. I sustained you for 40 days without solid food. Don't you think that I can start a church through you?"

God knew my hang-ups. I was afraid I was not capable of starting a church. I was afraid of moving my family away from doctors, family, and a good paying job. I was afraid that God would not provide the people or money.

But all along, God was saying and proving He could indeed do all that and more.

COUNT THE COST

Jesus said this in Luke: "Suppose one of you wants to build a tower. Won't you first sit down and estimate the cost to see if you have enough money to complete it? For if you lay the foundation and are not able to finish it, everyone who sees it will ridicule you, saying, 'This person began to build and wasn't able to finish'" (Luke 14:28-30).

In the same way, I believe Jesus wants you to count the cost by doing your own calculation. He wants you to seek Him. This is not necessarily time wasted but time invested in your faith journey.

Prayer time equals time invested in your faith journey. Sometimes it may seem like there are so many more pressing matters, but that is not the case. You must pray first. Maybe God is calling you to reach beyond your own selfish desires by leading your small group to reach out to the poor in your city, or lead your church into reaching more people far from God, or leading your family spiritually. Whatever the case, you must rely on God through prayer to empower you through His Spirit daily. Prayer is part of denying yourself.

The awesome twin of prayer is fasting. In that famous passage Matthew 6, Jesus said, "When you pray." Jesus also said, "When you fast." This implies to me that Jesus wants us not only to engage in praying, but also fasting.

I know that some people cannot go without food because of health reasons. That is okay. God is not down on you. Maybe there is something else you and your family can fast from: Internet, social media, or television. Just think of the money we could save by not eating out for a month so that we could help the poor and needy in our city or around the world.

As you pray, Jesus might ask you to fast from something. For me, it was food.

Here is what fasting mixed with prayer does:

Prayer and Fasting Put God in First Place

It is an automatic denial of self. When you take time not just to pray but to give up something and replace that with time with

God, you are automatically putting Him in first place in your life. This can be a leap out of our normal comfort.

It is not normal to put God in first place. It is not normal for people to stop eating for a period of time. Some might call this crazy.

When I was fasting, I still had to live life. I avoided being in groups going out to eat as much as possible, but sometimes it was unavoidable. I remember one particular time going to my favorite Mexican restaurant. I loved this place. If they could take an I.V. and hook me up to the salsa, I would be in heaven. I thought, "How in the world will I ever make it through this?"

A miracle occurred as I entered the restaurant: I could not smell the food. I couldn't believe it. As I put God first, He did a small miracle for me in that moment. Then as people started asking, I had to explain to them why I wasn't eating; I was fasting. The obvious next question was "How long?" When I said 40 days, the crazy looks and comments came!

You may want to start out slow. For example, only fast during lunch, or only during the day, or just a 24-hour period. Do NOT set out to do a 40-day or any type of extended fast without doctor supervision, a direct call from God, and some experience in fasting. With that said, you must understand that the faith God gives you during fasting is unbelievable.

Prayer and Fasting Release Greater Faith In Your Life.

When praying and fasting, my faith in God goes through the roof. I feel as though I can really do ALL things through Christ who gives me the strength! It unleashes faith in Jesus like nothing else. Maybe this is because food and normal routine in life can have a way of numbing our sensitivity to the spiritual things happening around us.

Prayer and Fasting Release Greater Witnessing Power in Your Life

After a time of prayer and fasting, I see my power to share Jesus to others compound. It is as if God gives me more opportunities to share His love with others. As you pray and fast, opportunities to talk about Jesus will open up. During this time, you will feel a special empowering to speak boldly for Jesus. Spend time in prayer and fasting and watch as He proves to you that He can do whatever He desires through you.

THEN WHAT?

What is Jesus asking you to do? You have prayed. You have fasted. You know beyond doubt that God is calling you. You have said yes. Now is the time to go.

For us, we put a map of the United States on our bedroom wall. We knew God wanted us to move to a growing area and a place where there were not many evangelical churches.

So I began to research. I looked at demographics of about 30 locations. I prayed and fasted some more.

Finally, one day while in prayer and fasting in my office, I wrote in my journal eight locations that Jesus brought to my mind. I went home and put thumbtacks on those locations. My wife and I began to pray.

HOW DO I KNOW THE VOICE OF GOD?

For me to flippantly write "Jesus brought to my mind" and not say more would do a disservice to you. Sometimes pastors use terms like *God spoke, Jesus said to me,* and *I was prompted* in ways that make the hearer think they are below par because they have not had the same experiences.

God speaks to us today. He has spoken through the Bible. This is God's Word to us. If any thought, voice, or dream you are having does not line up with the Bible, then it is not from God. We can get in trouble by just following every feeling, or even "voice" we have inside our hearts and head. The truth is that "All have sinned and fall short of the glory of God" (Romans 3:23). We all have this natural inclination to do what is evil. If we are not careful in discerning these "voices, promptings, or feelings" we will not be following Jesus' call but our own or even worse, the enemy's.

As I said earlier, there are several instances in the Bible where Jesus called people to follow Him, make disciples, and be His witnesses. God asks these very broad yet specific callings of every believer. So, in part, the voice of God has already spoken about reaching out to everyone with the gospel of Jesus Christ.

But even further than that, Jesus speaks to us through His Holy Spirit on a daily, ongoing basis.

I am going to be honest here: I have never heard an audible voice from God. But, the Holy Spirit does put calculated thoughts upon my mind that I know are from Him. These thoughts are not random. They are not even spontaneous. They are calculated because God has already calculated the plans for His kingdom and how I will participate in that.

How do I know these thoughts are from God?

The Holy Spirit Does NOT Go Against the Bible

The Holy Spirit is a part of the triune Godhead. This simply means that God the Father, the Son, and the Holy Spirit are three in one. They are together, yet separate persons. It can be hard to understand; however, this is one of those things we must accept by faith based on the Bible as well. Since the Bible is God's Word to us, you must understand that the Holy Spirit will never say or cause you to think something contrary to what the Bible says. The thoughts you have that are against the Bible are not from God. Either they are a product of your own sinful desires,

21

or the enemy is putting them there to distract you from what God really wants.

I Must Have an Ongoing Understanding of the Bible

As a believer in Jesus who wants to do what He says every day, listen, and obey His voice, I must have an ongoing understanding and relationship with the Bible. In other words, I must read it! Having a daily time where we read God's Word and seek to know what He is saying to us through it can solve the vast majority of our issues in our lives.

One of the main reasons why most Christ followers do not seek to live a life devoted to obeying what Jesus is asking them to do is because they are comfortable in their own false understanding of the Bible, which really is a product of never reading it on a consistent basis. If the Bible is God's Word to us, then we have to read it to be truly discerning of the many voices inside our heads. Do not be afraid to start reading it today. Do not let a lack of understanding every single verse stop you from reading it. The more you read it, the more you will start to understand and see God's voice to you in it.

Will Obeying This Thought Bring Me Out of My Comfort Zone?

This is not a foolproof question. You cannot start with this question. You must start with an ongoing understanding and relationship with the Bible. Then you can move to this question.

However, when God speaks, He usually is asking us to do something out of our comfort zone.

Shortly after moving to Yuma, I started meeting people and gathering a small group. One individual I met called me out of the blue to ask me to meet with him at a local restaurant. So I did. As this man began to pour out his heart to me, he confessed he was going through a deep, dark, depressing time. As he was speaking, I kid you not, a thought came to my mind: "We should go to the local post office and stand in the drive thru line and hand out FREE bottled water."

Say what? I quickly filtered this thought through: "Does this go against the Bible? Please Lord, let it be against the Bible or else I will look crazy asking this guy to do this with me!" The prospect of going and handing out bottles of water was not the crazy part. The crazy part was that I hardly knew this guy. I was concerned with what he thought more than obeying what God was asking of me.

After realizing this thought was not against the Bible, and knowing it definitely brought me out of my comfort, I knew I had to obey.

Does Obeying This Thought Help Fulfill the Great Commission and the Great Commandment?

Remember earlier I said that God has called all of us to some broad yet specific callings that are outlined in many passages throughout the Bible. Much of them have to do with what is called the *Great Commission* and the *Great Commandment*.

Here is an example of the Great Commission: "But you will receive power when the Holy Spirit comes on you; and you will be my witnesses in Jerusalem, and in all Judea and Samaria, and to the ends of the earth" (Acts 1:8). And the Great Commandment: "'Love the Lord your God with all your heart and with all your soul and with all your mind and with all your strength.' The second is this: 'Love your neighbor as yourself'" (Mark 12:30-31).

These two filters are what I call the final filters in counting the cost and determining whether the thought is from God.

As I quickly ran through these last filters in my mind, I realized that I must obey and mention this service opportunity to this man. So I said, "I got an idea. How about we go to the local grocery store and by two cases of bottled water and ice, swing by my house and pick up two coolers, and then go to the post office and hand out FREE bottled water?"

The crazy look that came from him was priceless. I really did not give him time to respond. I quickly got up and said, "Let's go!"

We hopped in my vehicle and drove to the local store. On the way, I called my wife and said, "Melissa, uh, I got Craig with me in the car. We are headed to the store to get two cases of bottled water and some ice. Can you have the coolers ready? We are going to the post office to hand out free bottled water."

The silence on the other end told me that she was quite worried about my sanity and safety. Again, the reason why she was worried is because she had no idea who this man was. The idea of passing out bottled water was not as crazy as going with someone I did not know and carrying out this act of kindness together. She paused, probably thought about my past behaviors and choices to jump first and ask questions later lifestyle , and said, "Okay."

By this time, I had convinced myself this was God's will; however, Craig was not so sure. He kept questioning me. So I said, "When I serve someone else with no strings attached, I always have joy in my heart." This man was experiencing some depression so I knew the joy of serving someone else would cheer him up. Whether I convinced him or not, he had two choices: Go through with this or jump out of the car and run! He chose the first. We bought the ice and water and loaded it up in the car. It seemed his attitude started to improve with just that small gesture. Then we headed to my house.

My lovely wife rolled up the garage door and rolled out the coolers while at the same time looking at me with that with a look of "who is this guy with you". I did not give her time to speak; we loaded up the coolers with water and ice, put them in the car, and drove to the post office.

24

We had some time to drive and allow the water to get cold. However, in Yuma, when it is a hot summer day and the temperature is well over 100 degrees, just cool water will do!

We set up camp at the drive thru. I told him he could wipe down the waters as they came out of the cooler, and I would do all the talking. He said, "What are you going to say?" My answer: "We are just doing this to show God's love today."

As the first few cars drove through, I watched as God turned his heart from being in depression to filling him with joy. The look of surprise on the driver's faces is what truly made a lasting impression. They drove up just expecting to drop off mail, maybe on their lunch break, or just a normal routine. However, there comfortable routine was shook up when two guys were standing there handing out free bottled water. It really is not about the water that was handed out. It is the act of stepping out of your comfortable routine while interrupting someone else's routine to show kindness. It only took about 30 minutes to hand out both cases. As we finished, there was a pep in his step now. He emptied out the remaining ice from the coolers, helped me pack them up, and hopped in the car. He said, "Jason, you know what we just did changed the whole perspective of my day and my outlook on life."

BOOM! The Holy Spirit knew what He was doing!

The small promptings through the thoughts the Holy Spirit puts in your mind are the voice of God to you. You must count the cost by doing your part and obeying. I am convinced that when we get a glimpse of God's love for us and truly how holy He is and out of that holiness He sent His son Jesus to die for us, then our fear of what others think, our stubbornness, and our disobedience will turn into full out obedience by faith to Him.

NEXT STEPS

1. What are some great acts of faith you recall from the Bible?
2. Has there ever been a time in your life where Jesus asked you to take a leap of faith?
3. If there were one thing you could do and knew you would not fail at it, what would it be?
4. Write down some "thoughts" the Holy Spirit has been placing on your mind that some might call crazy.
5. What steps do you need to take to "count the cost" to do "your part" in risking crazy?

CHAPTER 4

THE GREAT WORK INSIDE YOU

"Then he said to them all: 'Whoever wants to be my disciple must deny themselves and take up their cross daily and follow me" (Luke 9:23).

Living the risking crazy lifestyle is not only about having a daily surrender and denial of our selfish ways, but also continues as we "take up our cross daily." This is a curious thing.

In our minds when we hear the word *cross*, we think of Jesus dying on the cross. Did Jesus mean we literally would die a cruel, undeserved death on wooden beams daily? Obviously, the literal connotation of the word does not mean we will be crucified like Jesus. However, there is a sense of dying implied here. As I said before, denying our self is a form of dying to our selfishness, stubbornness, and disobedience. For most of us, this can be very cruel to our ego, pride, and reputation.

In addition to this denial of self, we need to pick up our own sort of cross. This Christian walk is much more than just praying a prayer or coming forward at an altar in a church service. The walk is one that will take every ounce of energy we have with undying focus on glorifying the Father in heaven with everything within us. And, it must be done daily.

So much of our life is focused on "me." What can I get out of it? Sometimes we even start out with the purest of motives, but quickly turn everything in our life into building ourselves up instead of loving God and loving others.

When praying about starting a church and moving across the country to Yuma, Arizona to do this, my immediate reactions were: What is in it for me? I covered them up with rational excuses like: Would my family be taken care of? I have a good paying job; why leave? I have to raise how much money? There is no reason to go off the deep end, is there?

Through the world's eyes around me, these were all valid excuses for not obeying God's call on my life. We all use these same seemingly valid excuses. Who does not want their family to be taken care of? Who is not concerned with having a good paying job? All of us have those excuses for rationalizing not obeying God's voice. However, as we have discussed, in God's eyes, it was simply disobedience not to "take up my cross" and then "follow Him."

Simply put—I was afraid. I had a high view of myself, my needs, and what others thought of me. To tell you that I obeyed immediately, packed our bags, and moved would be a lie. I had much to work through. It took me almost two years to finally announce to our little world that we were moving 1,700 miles away from everyone and everything we knew to start a church in Yuma, Arizona. (I often joke, "It is not the end of the world, but you can see it from here!")

As it turns out, this was the cross Jesus wanted me to bear daily. It would not be easy. As you will find out, we did not just show up and thousands flocked to hear my amazing preaching! It is and was tough. But, God taught me and is teaching me much through it.

Your cross may not be to overcome the fear of others and go start a church away from everyone and everything you know.

However, I do believe everyone has a cross to bear daily. When you start down this path of risking crazy—dedicated to taking risks—that some might call crazy—for Jesus—you will be asked by our great God to do GREAT things for Him daily.

For me, the greatness was not starting a church. The greatness was God's daily work on my heart leading me to take up my cross for Him. The cross that I had and still have to overcome daily is the fear of others.

THE DAY NO ONE CAME

I still remember that morning. Melissa and I were excited because we were expecting eight to 12 adults to come to our house and join us on a Sunday morning for what was to be the vision casting of a great church. Melissa prepared the house, had snacks, and got the kids prepared, while I prepared the vision message, along with PowerPoint on our television. I set out some chairs so we would have enough seats.

9:45 a.m. came and no one was there yet; however, never fear because in Yuma, it is natural to be late to everything. We were learning our culture and adapting. 9:55 a.m., no one came. 10:00 a.m., still no one. Again, not that unusual for Yuma, but by the time 10:30 a.m. rolled around and no one was there, we knew that no one was coming.

You cannot imagine the devastation I had in my heart. I was even afraid to look at Melissa. I remember going to the bedroom and just letting my body hit the bed with the weight of the world crashing with it. I knew what would happen about noon. My dad would phone and ask, "How many came?" Melissa's parents would call, knowing that their church along with others and many individuals were praying that day.

The questions in my mind were worse than any question from another person. Thoughts like: What have you done?

29

You're a failure! Even moments of self-pity that I dare not write in a book. It was one of the worst feelings in my life. I had moved my young family 1,700 miles from everyone...for this!

But what I was not realizing at the moment was this: God was already pleased with me. Will you read that again? *God was pleased with me.*

Because if you are going to choose daily to deny yourself and take up your cross, you will have moments where you feel like a total, complete loser and failure. I believe this might be part of the cross bearing.

What was my fear? Looking back, I can truly, deep-down tell you that I feared what others thought of me. The reality is though as a follower of Jesus Christ, you and I have already pleased God by putting our faith in Him.

God's measuring stick is perfect holiness, and you can never measure up. This is why He sent Jesus to die on the cross for your sins. Jesus met the demands of God's holiness to set us free from the fear of others—and all sin—so we could take up our cross for the glory of God. When you place your faith in Jesus, Jesus has met the standard for you. So relax.

Jesus is calling you to take that calculated risk that some might call crazy. You do not know all the details, it will not go as you planned, and you might even feel like you have failed at times. But the truth is that God is already pleased with you because you are taking the risk placed in you through your faith in Jesus.

The next 24 hours were a blur for me after that Sunday. The moment I remember was driving out to the desert and looking at a giant mountain in front of me. No one was around so I told God exactly how I felt. I told God that the mountain of starting this church was in front of me. I believed He could do it. I told Him that. I prayed, cried, and begged God to do something mighty.

I would like to tell you that the mountain crumbled before my eyes. I would like to say that after that, thousands of people came flocking to my house to hear the Word of God. I would like to say that the next few years were easy and it still is. None of that happened.

God showed up that day, but it was not in the form of the mountain crumbling, fire falling from heaven, or a heavy gust of wind. The Holy Spirit put this thought in my mind: "I love you, Jason. I have called you to do this. Trust in Me."

That truly is what kept me in Yuma. That voice inside my head, called the Holy Spirit, who spoke those words of love to me.

As you walk in faith, your daily cross will lead you back to those same words: "I love you and I have called you to do this. Trust in Me."

God had the plan calculated. God allowed me to go through that day when no one came. He knew that it would take four years to gather 100 people. He knew that we would have 54 on our first Sunday, and then I would grow it down to 18 in four months. He knew all of that. It was part of His grand plan to draw me closer to Himself.

Planting a church was not the great thing that was happening. The great thing that was happening was God's work inside me. The same is true for you. As you approach this lifestyle of taking risks, the great thing will not be a ministry, church, small group, or even godly children. Sure, all of those are great in the sense of lives being changed for Jesus. But the true great work will take place inside of you.

NEXT STEPS

1. What are some of the biggest fears that face our society today?
2. Which of those fears do you identify with?
3. When was a time in your life where you felt the love of God greatly?
4. Write out what you believe God thinks of you.
5. Memorize 2 Timothy 1:7.

CHAPTER 5

LISTEN TO THE CRIES OF THE NEEDY

My friend and partner in the ministry from Mexico, Jose Esparza, said this to me about the churches he has planted there. He said, "When we came to Mexico to spread the name of Jesus, we found out that many people had heard the gospel, but had never seen the gospel!" What a profound statement when talking about risking crazy, because Jesus has called those who believe in Him to be His hands and feet.

My friend and I both believe that the gospel must be preached. It must be shared with our words. However, I would also say that it must be shared with our hands and feet as well. To truly live out this lifestyle by denying yourself and taking up your cross, you must come to the conclusion that your cross as Christ followers must be that of living a life of generosity leading to the presentation of the gospel. This "cross" can come in many forms, including but not limited to, our time and our money.

We serve a God who was so generous that He gave us His Son, Jesus. He practiced this generosity. You might even say the cross that Jesus bore was generosity. He displayed this generosity by giving us life instead of death through belief in Him. If

God is generous through Jesus, surely He calls those who say they follow Him to be and do the same.

However, growing up in church, sitting in the pews, and serving on staff at churches, I have seen that "church people" can sometimes be less than generous. I have often wondered why? Why are we, who have been given freely so much, the ones who will so quickly hold on to what we have?

I believe we have a fear. Right after Jesus said, "Deny yourself, and take up your cross," He said this: "For whoever wants to save their life will lose it, but whoever loses their life for me will save it. What good is it for someone to gain the whole world, and yet lose or forfeit their very self?" (Luke 9:24-25).

There is a generous exchange that must take place. You must generously give your life back to the one who generously gave His. As you do this, your life is no longer your own, but His. So He comes along and asks you to move beyond your normal routines of life and take steps of faith for Him.

WE MUST START LISTENING TO THE CRIES OF OUR CITY

It is my belief that the poor and needy of our cities are crying out to God, whether they have a faith in Jesus or not. They are asking God to save them from their worldly based circumstances—lack of food, no money, abuse, or sickness.

God is listening. Look at what He says in Psalm 69:33, "The LORD hears the needy and does not despise his captive people" (Psalm 69:33).

Sometimes we think that God may be hearing, but not really listening. I have been guilty of this when talking with my wife. She can pick up on it really quick. I am hearing her voice, but I have no idea what she said. I can assure you that God is not that way. He listens, hears, and then calls you and I to action. Could it be that the reason we think God is not listening is because the action is supposed to come from Him through us?

In our little pocket of the world,, God was calling me to action. I vividly remember the prompting of the Spirit not only to fill some seats, but also to fill needs in our city! Many might argue that just giving people a blanket for their cold bodies, or some cold water for their thirsty tongues, is not sharing the gospel. I would somewhat agree. I would agree that it is not fully sharing the gospel of Jesus dying for their sins and that they need a relationship with Him. However, it is showing the generosity of Jesus through you and therefore giving you an opportunity to share the Word of the gospel with them. People need to see the gospel in action through your life of sacrificial generosity for Jesus.

As God began to put on my heart that the church needed to be the hands and feet of Jesus, we kept asking the question, how? I remember making a commitment to God. It went something like this, "God, reveal to me each moment of every day how to be generous, and I will obey." This prayer became a bold prayer for me.

What I found out was that the needy in our city were praying, "God please help," while at the same time, I was asking God to show me where to help. Guess what? God showed me.

On one particular hot day, we received a phone call from a lady. Danny Wells, our now executive pastor, fielded the call. After he spoke to her on the phone, he turned to me and said, "I told her we would go see her."

We pulled into the Motel 6 and looked for room 169. Two pastors knocking on a hotel door was not a good picture, but we were assured that her husband would be there. After a couple of knocks, her husband came to the door. We told him we were from the church; he let us in.

When the door to that room opened, the door to my heart opened. The prayer I had been praying came in my mind as I witnessed two people who were really crying out to God for help. We really were the answer for that moment. The room was filled with all their belongings. There was a small bed in the room in which she was not only sleeping, but stayed in all day. She was bed ridden and her husband would sleep on the floor. Tears flooded her eyes as she realized that her prayers had been answered and someone finally came to see them. I found out she had called many churches. No one came. We were it. God had made our worlds collide at that moment.

What we did for them fails in comparison to what happened to our hearts. We ended up spending all kinds of money to help this couple get back on their feet. We realized this was just a small snapshot of the needy in our city. As we continually kept praying for God to use us and show us needs, He kept opening doors to opportunities.

Helping that couple meant we had to spend hours in the hot summer sun working on his R.V. It meant many more phone calls from them needing help. It meant getting out of our office and being the hands and feet of Jesus. It meant giving sacrificially of our finances as a church. It caused us to ask some questions: What were we really building? Was it just an organization, or an organism that would be the hands and feet of Jesus? What are the other needs in our city? How were we going to fund these things?

As a church, we knew that we had not only to spread the gospel by the spoken Word, but also by the actions in our everyday life.

During budget planning meetings at churches every year, this question is asked: How are we going to get by? But why not ask: "What needs does God want us to fill in the coming year?

Sure, there has to be wisdom in budget planning. We have to pay certain bills.

But what about faith? What about mission? What about taking those risks that God is asking of you? Are there people crying out in your city? Who will meet their needs? I believe Jesus is calling you. I believe Jesus is calling me. How will we respond?

PRACTICE GENEROSITY

Generosity is the cure to the fear of not enough. But being generous is risky.

Think about this: A holy God in heaven saw His creation constantly turning their backs on Him and disobeying. He could have chosen to destroy it all and start over. Of course, the story of the flood in Noah's day is an account of the human race being destroyed, save one person and his family. Even in the midst of God's holy wrath toward humanity, He chose to save Noah. But that is not the end of the story. We read all throughout the Old Testament how God was on a saving redeeming mission to bring people back to Himself.

In the single most generous act ever, God sent His son, Jesus. As we look at the life of Jesus, we see that His entire life was controlled by sacrifice and generosity. God chose to save humanity once and for all through the sacrifice and generous gift of His Son. His Son chose generously to lay down His life for the sins of humanity.

When we truly grasp what God has done for us through Jesus Christ, then we will be spurred on to good works that ultimately glorify Him. I struggle with the fear of not enough when my heart turns from the cross of Jesus to myself. However, we have all that we need through Jesus. He is enough. Waking up each day with this realization will lead us to a life of generosity.

37

Shortly after helping this couple out in various ways, we realized that the mission of our church was truly to be the hands and feet of Jesus. We created what is now called our "Mercy Ministry."

This ministry is built on nothing but showing mercy to those in need in our city. Using prudent and wise budgeting measures built in with risk, we decided to take a percentage of our Sunday morning offering and use it in this ministry to meet the needs of those crying out to God for help in our city. Since then, by the grace of God, we have been able to spend thousands of dollars helping those in need in our city.

What if we looked at the people in our city as Jesus did? Do you remember this verse? "When he saw the crowds, he had compassion on them, because they were harassed and helpless, like sheep without a shepherd" (Matthew 9:36).

What Jesus said in that verse included all the people. It was not just the ones He was comfortable with. "Harassed, helpless, and like sheep without a shepherd" were the words He used to describe the crowds of people He saw.

The very next words of Jesus are the call to action: "Then he said to his disciples, 'The harvest is plentiful but the workers are few. Ask the Lord of the harvest, therefore, to send out workers into his harvest field'" (Matthew 9:37-38).

There is a great harvest of people who are "harassed, helpless, and like sheep without a shepherd." The question is what are we going to do about it? Jesus in this moment is talking to the disciples.

Are you a disciple of Jesus? He is talking to you and me.

Some might stop and say, but He said, "pray" that God would send workers. He did say that, but in the next chapter, Matthew 10, Jesus sends out the 12 disciples.

We can pray and ask God where the needs are and who needs to go; however, the prayer needs to change quickly from "who" to "I will go."

NEXT STEPS

1. Who are the "harassed, helpless, and sheep without a shepherd" in your city?
2. Do ever feel like you do not have enough time, talent, or even money to help fill needs in your city?
3. What are some ways you can start, as a family, filling a need of those crying out to God for help in your city?
4. As a small group, spend some time in prayer asking God to open your eyes to see the needs around you.
5. As God opens the eyes of your heart to the needs around you, ask Him to show you practical ways to meet those needs.
6. Start making a list of ways you as a family, church, or small group can take financial resources and meet some needs in your city.

CHAPTER 6

GENEROSITY LEADS TO REPENTANCE

I will never forget the day, when Miss Kay came to our church for the first time. She got out of her car, opened the back of her trunk, pulled out a hover-round wheel chair, and drove herself up the sidewalk and into the school where we were meeting. Miss Kay was much older than our small congregation was, and I wondered if she liked our style of service. I remember preaching and looking at her as she listened intently.

After the service was over, she made a decision to follow Jesus. As I helped her back to her car and we loaded the mechanical wheelchair back into the trunk of her car, I asked her a question: What made you choose to come to The Vertical Church?

To tell you the truth, I was dumbfounded that she had found her way to the school where we were meeting. We had mailed postcards, done some advertising, etc., but none of them went to her neighborhood. We had maybe 50-60 people attending our church, and none of them knew her. We had new people come to our church almost weekly, but they usually had some sort of connection.

Miss Kay said, "I heard about your church through reading about all the kind things that your church has been doing to help the needy in our city." She went on to say, "In all my life, I had never seen a church actually use the money that was given to really help real people in real need. That is what drew me here." I found out later that it took her over an hour to find our church that day, but by the grace of God, she made it.

Jesus confirmed to me that day that generosity really does lead people to repentance. That He can use us to show people the gospel while at the same time giving us the opportunity to tell them the gospel. This risking crazy lifestyle really is worth it.

You see, Miss Kay, had never received any aid from our church; she had never received a bottle of water from us; and she had never received any type of random act of generosity from our church. But, she had heard about it. That is amazing.

I will never forget the day we baptized Miss Kay. It was a monumental day for her even to get into the pool. About a month later, she breathed her last breath and met Jesus face to face. We found out through her death that she did not have anybody. No one. She was living alone and had been for years with no family—none. My wife and a few other women from church were the only ones who visited her in those last days.

God used our risk taking adventures in our city to touch Miss Kay's heart enough to lead her to our church where she heard the gospel and gave her life to Jesus. But not only that, she gained a family that cared for her.

START SMALL

How did we get to that point? We started small. We started with room 169 where the couple lived. It started with us deciding that we would deny our self and take up our cross daily. It started small. It started with "loving your neighbor as your self." It started with a conscious decision, fueled by the Holy Spirit, to desire to see God's will to be worked out in every avenue of our life.

What is God asking of you today? I am not talking about to-morrow, a year from now, or five years from now. Today.

The simple obedience from day-to-day leads us to taking those giant leaps of faith. What if you set a goal to touch one life a day? What if you started praying, "Lord, help me to be gener-ous today"? How would your life change? How would the lives around you change?

Is this not what we as the body of Christ are supposed to do? Are we not to be generous as our heavenly Father is generous? We could never match the generosity of God displayed by Him giving us Jesus; however, we can live daily in this attitude of generosity. Generosity does make a difference in people's lives. It does give you and I opportunities to speak Jesus to those far from Him.

In the last chapter of Colossians, Paul gave final instruc-tions to the church at Colossae. He starts in verse two by saying: "Devote yourselves to prayer, being watchful and thankful. And pray for us, too, that God may open a door for our message, so that we may proclaim the mystery of Christ, for which I am in chains" (Colossians 4:2-3).

The implication is that as we devote ourselves to prayer, God will open doors for the message. Paul was in "chains" because of this message. He was daily taking up his cross for Jesus. He was one of the early risk takers.

As I stated earlier, prayer and communicating with God is the way you know what risks He is asking you to take. Hearing and obeying His voice is a key for living out God's daily call of faith in your life.

After Paul was well into his life's work for Christ, he asked the Colossians to: "Pray that I may proclaim it clearly, as I should?" (Colossians 4:4).

There is much noise in our lives that cloud out the mes-sage of the gospel. Sometimes as Christians, we bring this on ourselves. People tend to hear us shouting about what we are against while missing the message of what we are for. Paul says the prayer should be that the message is proclaimed clearly. I believe generosity clears up the message of the gospel.

As we start in small ways every day obeying and practicing generosity toward others, then the message can be received clearly. Paul went on to say: "Be wise in the way that you act toward outsiders; make the most of every opportunity" (Colossians 4:5).

When we obey God's voice in these small areas by reaching beyond our self and practicing generosity, people are watching us; lives are being touched! Our job is not to dictate the results, but to leave those results up to God. He is the one in complete control of every situation and brings people unto Himself. He has called you and me to just "GO!"

NEXT STEPS

1. Describe a time in your life when you prayed for one thing, but God did something else.
2. Looking back on that time, was there a specific lesson or result that God was teaching you?
3. Knowing what you know now, would you be willing to pray bold prayers daily such as, "Lord, show me how to be generous today"?
4. What does "taking up your cross" mean for you?
5. What are some small, daily practical ways that you can start practicing generosity and kindness?
6. Write down three names that you will ask to join you on this risking crazy journey. Ask them to pray daily with you and for you, and then meet once a week to talk about how God is leading you in generosity.

CHAPTER 7

THE FASTEST MIRACLE EVER

Gathering the first 100 people as a small church plant was very difficult. In fact, it took us four years. I love to hear those stories where the planter shows up in a city, has a service and 500 people come the first week. This was not the case for us. I would dare say that it is not the case for the majority of church plants.

There was one thing that kept us going: Faith. We really believed God had called us to keep denying our self and taking up our cross. But, the real faith comes when we continue in this walk by "following Him" daily. It seems that I have always had an abundance of faith. Some might call it a spiritual gift; however, I really believe that God gives us all the same Spirit that produces the same faith. If I were to sugarcoat it, I would say that I have never faltered in my faith. But then that would be a lie. One thing I know, where I have known that God was calling and by faith I went, God has blessed.

FAITH PRECEDES THE MIRACLE

After those four years of setting up and tearing down a portable church in 115-degree weather in Yuma, we really felt drawn to be looking for a semi-permanent place to have church.

Shortly after arriving in Yuma, I began looking for a place to meet as a church. At that time, the old "Mandarin Cinema" was still playing movies. My plan was to meet with the owner and ask if we could meet there on Sunday before the movies started. I tried to meet with the owner, called the theater, left messages, and nothing. I remember one day sitting in the parking lot and praying, "God please let us meet in this building."

Fast-forward four years, the movie theater went out of business. Danny and I were out driving one day just looking for a place to meet and God drew us back to that building. We got out of the car and noticed a "lien notice" on the door. The good news was that the notice had a phone number on it. Before we called it, we wondered what a 15,000 square foot building would rent for. Actually, we knew because we had been looking. At that time, it was about a dollar per square foot per month. So a building that size would lease for about $15,000 a month.

Fear quickly swept in. There was no way we could afford that. We did not even have $15,000 in our bank account. We were currently paying $400 a month at the school. We looked at our finances and knew that we could not afford very much more than that. Danny and I finally settled on a number: $4,000. We were going to offer the owner $4,000 a month to lease the building. This was a very long shot! I still remember the sinking feeling in my stomach as Danny dialed the number.

Danny called and the owner answered. The question came out of Danny's mouth, "How much do you want to lease the old Mandarin Cinema building in Yuma?"

Danny's eyes got really big. I knew at that moment, it was out of our price range. What I found out later was that he wanted $8,000 a month. The next words out of Danny's mouth were, "Well, we can give you $4,000." Pause.

He said, "Well, I'll take it!" He went on to say how that the lease would be month to month, and the for-sale sign would stay out as well as it would still be on the market to rent.

Before Danny gave him our final answer, we had to get some keys to look at it as well as talk to some of those on our leadership team to see what they thought. After Danny hung up, I told him he should have offered him $3,000.

Over the next couple of days, we got the keys, looked it over, called the electric company to find out how much it would cost to turn on the electricity, as well as had our lawyer look over the lease agreement.

What happened next was one of the most faith-filled moments of my life. We gathered our leadership team in the darkened theater on the far end of the building. With the back door propped open for light, our families gathered as I cast the vision of what I thought God wanted us to do. I truly believed that God was leading us in this direction, to step out in faith, to deny our self, take up our cross, and follow Him.

I told them how awesome it would be to see the place filled with people every week coming to know Jesus. I told them the price and the stretch that would be, then I said, "By the way, we called the Electric Company and they want $13,000 to just turn on the electricity!" Nobody said anything.

So I gathered them in a circle with our kids and we all held hands. I prayed, "God, we need a miracle. We believe you want us in this building. But, we need $13,000 and we need it fast! We ask this and believe You for it, in Jesus name, Amen." We closed the back door, got our flashlights out, and walked out the front door.

As I was putting the key in the front door of my house, my cell phone rang. It was a pastor friend of mine in California.

"Jason," he said.

"Yes," I replied.

"Our board just voted to send you guys $6,500. We had some extra money at the end of the quarter and thought of you guys. Would that be alright?"

"Would that be alright?" I said, "You wait until I tell you what just happened!" I told him the story and with that hung up the phone.

I turned to my wife and two kids and told them about the conversation I just had on the phone. My son immediately without hesitation said, "That was the fastest miracle ever!" I replied, "Yes, it was." Within the next 24 hours, we had over $13,000 committed!

Faith always preceded miracles in the Bible. I believe it is true today. I am not endorsing a "word-faith" type theology. When we join ourselves with the work He is doing around us, miracles happen.

What kind of faith step is God asking you to take? It is time we start turning our attention toward actually following Him by following through with what He has called us to do. It is a daily denial of self, followed by great generosity mixed with faith-filled steps. There are many steps. All along the journey with Christ, He calls us continually to take step after step after step.

AS YOU FOLLOW, THE ENEMY WANTS TO DISTRACT YOU

As you follow, your enemy, Satan, is alive and well. He wants to do so much damage to God's plan in your life that you sometimes do not even know it is coming. Jesus said this:

"The thief comes only to steal and kill and destroy; I have come that they may have life, and have it to the full" (John 10:10).

All along this faith-filled journey, the thief, wants to steal, kill, destroy, and distract you from what God wants. For us, the

$13,000 could have become a distraction. Instead, we faithfully turned it over to God while trusting that somehow, someway He would take care of it. There were many more distractions to come for us in the weeks leading up to moving into the building. On one day, as we had already been working on the building for a couple of weeks, the owner shows up with a potential buyer and toured the building. I was terrified that this was it. We would be looking for another place. I walked around with him showing him all the things wrong with the building while praying that God would intervene. He did. The guy did not buy the building.

Following Him by faith means you have to deal with all the distractions. Your distractions will be different than mine. The enemy knows what will really get to us and paralyze our forward faith motion. Here are some ways to deal with distractions.

Remember Who Called You

You are called by God to do what you are doing. You may not be a pastor or missionary or church planter, but you are called. You are called to change the world. The God who called you also created the heavens and the earth. He is the one who raised Jesus from the dead. Oh, and by the way, that same Spirit that raised Jesus from the dead lives in you. You have to remember who called you. You have to look beyond the distraction and fear of failure. You have to have faith on the not so faith-filled days as well as the mountain top experiences.

Remember the Faith-filled Heroes of the Bible

My mind immediately goes back to Hebrews chapter 11, sometimes called, "God's Hall of Faith." In this chapter, we read about heroes, some named and some not, who had such faith that we cannot even fathom it. Remember those were real people like you and I. God called, they denied themselves, took up their cross and with faith followed Him. They were real live flesh and bone. Hebrews 12:1-3 is a continuation of chapter 11. It starts out by saying, "Therefore, since we are surrounded by such a great cloud of witnesses, let us throw off everything that hinders us and the sin that so easily entangles. And let us run with perseverance the race marked out for us" (Hebrews 12:1).

The implication is that these real live flesh and bone people we just read about in chapter 11 are in this "cloud of witnesses." They are saying, "If we can make it, you can too!" The writer further tells us about the distractions that are to come. He speaks of how they will "easily entangle us." We are to be on the lookout by throwing off these distractions. Remembering those who have gone on before us, helps with that. In addition to this, we need to...

Remember Jesus Who Is Already Pleased With Us

The writer in Hebrews goes on to say this: "Fixing our eyes on Jesus, the pioneer and perfecter of faith. For the joy that was set before him he endured the cross, scorning its shame, and sat down at the right hand of the throne of God" (Hebrews 12:2).

By looking to Jesus and remembering His example, we can see the one who "perfects faith." He is the perfect example. He is the better Enoch, Noah, Abraham, Sarah, Jacob, Joseph, Moses, and David. Jesus is the "perfecter of faith." He is the one who shows us perfect faith going beyond all the distractions and following the Father all the way to the cross.

This is awesome news. The truth that Jesus thought it was great joy to suffer, bleed, and die for us tells me that through Him nothing is impossible. He is "sat down at the right hand of the throne of God." This means that His work is done. When we accept Jesus into our lives, the payment for our sins is complete. He is sitting down. When He said, "It is finished." It was done. By putting our faith in Him for the forgiveness of our sins, we can know and walk in the fact that God is now pleased with us. Hebrews 11:6 says this: "And without faith it is impossible to please God, because anyone who comes to him must believe that he exists and that he rewards those who earnestly seek him" (Hebrews 11:6).

Have you put your faith in Jesus? If the answer is "Yes," then you have nothing to fear. You are already under the blood and God is already pleased with you. Whatever is holding you back from following Him is nothing but a distraction from the thief. It is a lie from Satan. You must combat him with these truths. The battle is never over until we stand before God and enter His kingdom. But the battle is already won through Jesus Christ. We must believe and have faith to move past the distraction.

As you begin to walk in the natural outflow of obedience, your faith will be stretched and Jesus will ask you to believe the impossible for His glory. Through this, you will see things done in your life and others that have eternal significance.

Remember how I said it took four years to gather 100 people? In just a few short months after moving into the building, God grew us by an additional 100 people over the period of just 3 weeks!

I often wonder how many lives are not being changed because people are allowing fear and distraction to paralyze them. I wonder how many people sit in church services week after week knowing deep down that God is moving them to practice generosity, or show mercy, or fill a need in another person's life but continually say, "No!" I wonder what God thinks of that. I know He loves us and nothing can separate us from that love. However, I wonder what we miss out on because of our disobedience?

I have to battle this all the time. Still today, Jesus asks me to do things and I baulk at the task. I often ignore that still small prompting in my mind to talk to that stranger. I sometimes argue with God in line at Starbucks when He is telling me to buy the person's drink behind me and then tell them why. I wonder what miracles are not happening because I am not full of faith but fear. What about you? What is God asking you to do today? It may not be a $13,000 step of faith, but it may be a kid from Compassion International, or a homeless person you pass every day. It may be a "Miss Kay" or a position that needs your help at the local soup kitchen.

What about your local church? Is part of the reason why your church is not reaching people far from God is because you are not involved in building relationships with those far from God? People all around us are searching for real love. The only real love that is out there is found in Jesus. But every day, men and women are losing hope there is a God that truly does love them. They see our infighting and our disunity and think, "If they cannot even get along among themselves, then maybe there is nothing to this man, Jesus."

I am convinced that God is speaking, calling, and tapping people on the shoulder, not just the ones who answer the call to "full time Christian service" like pastors and missionaries. He is calling all of His followers to be His hands and feet. We are just not following Him. We have a "personal" relationship with Jesus without joining the corporate body to help change the world around us. There are many social justice causes and issues out there, but if they are not done in the name of Jesus then all we are doing is providing a blanket. We need to provide a blanket as well as the gospel. Following Him means filling the need as well as sharing the gospel.

Following Him makes an eternal difference. Following Him requires faith. Here are a few examples from Jesus:

> "He replied, 'Because you have so little faith. Truly I tell you, if you have faith as small as a mustard seed, you can say to this mountain, 'Move from here to there,' and

it will move. Nothing will be impossible for you" (Matthew 17:20).

Amazing. Nothing will be impossible. What about this one:

"Jesus replied, 'Truly I tell you, if you have faith and do not doubt, not only can you do what was done to the fig tree, but also you can say to this mountain, 'Go throw yourself into the sea' and it will be done. If you believe, you will receive whatever you ask for in prayer'" (Matthew 21:21-22).

Believe in prayer. Prayer and faith go hand in hand. Whenever you get distracted or feel like you cannot follow through with Him, then pray. There is power in faith-filled prayer. Here is another example:

"Immediately Jesus reached out his hand and caught him. 'You of little faith,' he said, 'why did you doubt?'" (Matthew 14:31).

This was right after Peter walked on water. The faith that Peter had in Jesus that outweighed the faith of the others in the boat helped Peter do what has never been done since— walk on water!

Look at what Jesus said to a woman asking Him to heal his daughter:

"Then Jesus said to her, 'Woman, you have great faith! Your request is granted.' And her daughter was healed at that moment" (Matthew 15:28).

Maybe you heard the story about the man who was let down through the roof of a house to get to Jesus. The house was so crowded there was no way to get the paralyzed man through the front door and in front of Jesus. So his friends cared so much and believe that Jesus could heal their friend that they climbed on the roof with him and broke through the roof and lowered him down to Jesus. Look what Jesus did:

"Some men brought to him a paralyzed man, lying on a mat. When Jesus saw their faith, he said to the man, 'Take heart, son; your sins are forgiven'" (Matthew 9:2).

I want you to notice that it was because of "their" faith, that this man was forgiven and then healed.

What about your faith? Are you practicing faith-filled following? Jesus was serious about faith. These are just a few instances in Matthew. This is just one gospel. The rest of the New Testament speaks of faith in a great God who can do the impossible. He calls on you and I to believe that and to follow Him through and by that faith.

NEXT STEPS

1. What do you believe is the number one distraction that causes people not to walk in faith?
2. Think about and discuss with someone else the differences in the New Testament church we read about and in the church you attend today.
3. Describe ways to move beyond the distractions that are plaguing you.
4. Take time to meditate on the forgiveness that Jesus gives us.
5. What would it look like if you and others joined together to live out faith on a daily basis?
6. Will you commit to obey in faith what Jesus is asking you to do today?

CHAPTER 8

EMPOWER OTHERS TO RISK CRAZY

When you and I show great faith in a great God who can do great things, then our "following of Jesus" in turn produces fruit in the form of others around us taking up the torch to risk crazy.

I will never forget the week I came back from vacation and there was a man on the front porch of our church. It was not uncommon to show up to the building and find people outside. Sometimes people would want help with a utility bill. Or maybe they needed some food. We usually try to help in some way. Of course, we are not able to help every situation out; but, for the most part, we figure out how to fill needs.

While I was on vacation, Brent showed up on our front porch. Jeremy Dillman, our Worship Pastor, was there to greet him. Jeremy befriended Brent. Brent has some mental health issues and on top of that, he was homeless. Through our church, Jeremy became a follower of Jesus. He watched our church take risks for Jesus. He watched us truly care as much as we could for the poor. By watching us, he was inspired to take Brent under his wing to help as much as possible.

Immediately Brent started living on the front porch of our church. The police would question him at night, so we gave him a "security tag." I know what you're thinking, "That's a pretty big risk giving a mentally ill man a security tag." The truth is that by him being on our front porch and making rounds around the building, he warded off any body that would have had any intentions of doing illegal activity. Jeremy was taking a risk. Danny, our Executive Pastor, joined him on this venture. Together, they were following the call of Jesus on their hearts to reach out to this man. Brent later told Jeremy, "You know, you guys are the only ones in my life who didn't just 'one time' me." Jeremy inquired, what is "one-timed." Brent responded, "People have always helped me out 'one-time' and then told me to move on or had nothing else to do with me."

After I heard that, I realized that is exactly what we sometimes do as Christians. We "one time" people. The fact is that it was hard for Danny and Jeremy and eventually our church to embrace Brent living on our doorstep, taking baths in our bathroom, and talking to himself in our lobby on Sunday mornings. But those who take risks—that some might call crazy—for Jesus go beyond the "one time." They keep giving over and over again. When you start doing that, people watch and they are empowered to do more, serve others above themselves, and follow Jesus no matter what He says. Jeremy was empowered to do more because he was a part of a church that had at its heart to be the hands and feet of Jesus at all costs.

Over the course of several months, Danny started to dive deeper into Brent's personal life to see how we could help him get off the streets. Summer was coming in Yuma and our front porch was not place to spend the summer in scorching heat. Through really getting into Brent's life, we were able to find out that through some government help; Brent could possibly have a place to live. After several calls to potential apartments, trailers, etc., Danny found a place for Brent to live. So just before the summer hit, Brent moved into his own place where he lives today.

Danny and Jeremy have continued their relationship with Brent. When you start helping people out, don't plan on just "one timing" them. There have been many occasions where we have had to step in and help Brent repeatedly. We had a birthday party for him a few months ago at my house. Everyone brought gifts and Brent was the center of attention. He told us that night that he never thought he would ever feel welcomed into a church, but now he does. Just so you know, on occasion, Brent was the voice of The Vertical Church podcast! Before we moved to video Brent did the introduction to our weekly podcast.

Through denying yourself, taking up your cross, and following Him, others watch what you are doing inside the church and they are empowered to do the same. Who is that person in your church that needs to step up and listen to the cries of the needy in your city? Who is the person in your church that needs to follow Jesus no matter where He leads? The answer to these questions is you. Before you point to someone else, look in the mirror.

Our problem is that we do not feel qualified to empower others.

YOU ARE EMPOWERED TO EMPOWER OTHERS

You have life through the Holy Spirit within you! I love how the Apostle Paul starts out Romans 8. He says, "Therefore, there is now no condemnation for those who are in Christ Jesus, because through Christ Jesus the law of the Spirit who gives life has set you free from the law of sin and death" (Romans 8:1-2).

If you back up a chapter, Paul describes in chapter 7 an internal struggle that I believe all of us have. He says, "For I know that good itself does not dwell in me, that is, in my sinful nature.

For I have the desire to do what is good, but I cannot carry it out. For I do not do the good I want to do, but the evil I do not want to do—this I keep on doing" (Romans 7:18-19).

I know the context of this is talking about sin and the law; however, I think we can apply this to our following Jesus in everything. I think you would agree with me that there is much good that Jesus calls us to do, but, we have an easier time choosing the evil or meaningless thing to do than the good.

We have this same internal struggle that the Apostle Paul had. Chapter 8 of Romans is a continuation of the same thought. However, he gives us a great promise of God. He says, "There is now no condemnation for those in Christ Jesus.".

You may believe that you are just a regular church member that has nothing to offer. Maybe you believe that it is the pastor and leaders job to formulate this plan. As a pastor, I must confess that I would be thrilled for people just like you to come to me and tell me your plan to help lead people in taking risks for Jesus through the church. God may very well be leading you to start a risking crazy revolution in your church. God understands your struggle. He knows that when we are left to choose, we will choose evil; however, He has given us "the law of the Spirit" who gives us life and sets us free from this struggle. I think what Paul is saying here is just give up! Realize that you cannot do good on your own. However, through the Holy Spirit inside of you, you have been empowered to empower others.

The Holy Spirit inside of the believer is the great power source to do anything in which Jesus calls you to do. Anything is possible through Him. We forget that we have a great resource that is God inside of us. When you think you are inadequate or unworthy, remember that deep down you are, but He who lives in you is greater than that. Paul goes on to write this in Romans 8: "You, however, are not in the realm of the flesh but are in the realm of the Spirit, if indeed the Spirit of God lives in you. And if anyone does not have the Spirit of Christ, they do not belong to Christ" (Romans 8:9).

Paul is not questioning your salvation here. I believe he is reiterating the fact that when you place your faith in Jesus, He gives you the "Spirit of Christ." He gives you the Holy Spirit. The Holy Spirit baptizes you into Jesus at salvation and then Jesus baptizes you into the Holy Spirit simultaneously. We could get mixed up on words here, but the bottom line is as a follower of Jesus, you have the Spirit inside of you at the moment of salvation.

Paul is saying you are in a different "realm." It is a spiritual realm. As you look into the mirror, you see the physical, but God when He looks at you, He sees the seal of the Holy Spirit upon your soul, and that gives you the power to do all He asks. He goes on to say in verse 11:

"And if the Spirit of him who raised Jesus from the dead is living in you, he who raised Christ from the dead will also give life to your mortal bodies because of his Spirit who lives in you" (Romans 8:11).

Did you read that? The same Spirit that raised Jesus from the dead lives inside of the believer. Your power is of the spiritual realm found in Jesus Christ through the Holy Spirit. If that same Spirit lives in you who raised Jesus from the dead, do you not think that you can do what Jesus is asking?

You are empowered to empower others. They are empowered by watching you step out of your comfort and take leaps of faith. My suggestion is to not wait on your pastor, small group leader, or friends to start risking crazy. You need to step out of the boat of comfort today. Start small, ask Jesus to show you who to touch with kindness, then follow Him. Just in case you need more convincing, let's read on in Romans 8. Paul writes: "What, then, shall we say in response to these things? If God is for us, who can be against us?" (Romans 8:31).

God is for you. In Christ, you have already pleased God. You have nothing or no one against you. If you feel condemned, it is not from God. It is either an internal struggle or the enemy is truly attacking you. When we get to a place where we realize that we are nothing on our own and cannot save ourselves or do true good on our own, then we will be willing to embrace the love of a Savior who offers us free grace and free salvation. This offer of free grace empowers us through the Spirit to carry out His plans in this world. Paul continues: "He who did not spare his own Son, but gave him up for us all—how will he not also, along with him, graciously give us all things?" (Romans 8:32)

You need help in this faith-filled lifestyle? Look to the One who gave His only Son for you. The only thing that gets Danny and Jeremy through this ongoing up and down relationship with Brent is knowing that the God who did not spare us His son will give us all things.

If you are like me, you may be somewhat convinced that you can do this and empower others to risk crazy. But as we go and be the hands and feet of Jesus, we will hear that condemning voice again. But remember: "Who will bring any charge against those whom God has chosen? It is God who justifies. Who then is the one who condemns? No one. Christ Jesus who died— more than that, who was raised to life—is at the right hand of God and is also interceding for us" (Romans 8:33-34).

No one condemns you. Stop listening to those voices inside of you that says, "You can never do anything for Jesus." Jesus who died and was raised up is not condemning you. He is "interceding" for you. Which means He is making a way for you. He did not leave you alone to take these steps. He does not call you to follow without the power to do so. No! He gives you The Holy Spirit to empower you to empower others.

Paul ends this chapter with this great statement: "Who shall separate us from the love of Christ? Shall trouble or hardship or persecution or famine or nakedness or danger or sword? As it is written: 'For your sake we face death all day long: we are considered as sheep to be slaughtered.' No, in all these things we are more than conquerors through him who loved us. For I am convinced that neither death nor life, neither angels nor demons, neither the present nor the future, nor any powers, neither height nor depth, nor anything else in all creation, will be able to separate us from the love of God that is in Christ Jesus our Lord" (Romans 8:35-39).

That statement pretty much covers everything. The early church was facing real persecution. If they were able to get through all of those hardships, do you not think that through the power of Jesus in us through His Spirit, we can do all that He asks of us and follow Him? I think so. Paul tells us we can. You are empowered to empower others. But you have to start. You have to get up and follow Him.

NEXT STEPS

1. Name three people who have inspired you to take risks for Jesus.
2. What characteristics do they have that you believe caused them to step in great faith?
3. Looking inside of you, what is it that you feel is holding you back from following Jesus' next steps for your life?
4. In what ways do you identify with the Apostle Paul in Romans chapter 7?
5. Write down three faith promises from God's Word that will encourage you to take risks for Him.
6. Write out a plan to touch one person with the love of Christ for the next 6 weeks.

CHAPTER 9

Taking Risking Crazy to Another Level

When Jesus taps us on the shoulder and asks us to deny our self, take up our cross and then follow Him, His plans are far greater than we could ever imagine on our own. The apostle Paul says it like this: "Now to him who is able to do immeasurably more than all we ask or imagine, according to his power that is at work within us, to him be glory in the church and in Christ Jesus throughout all generations, for ever and ever! Amen" (Ephesians 3:20-21).

This is the ending to a prayer for the Church at Ephesus. His prayer is pointing toward heaven and challenging the reader that God can do more than we could ever dream of.

When we began The Vertical Church, my goal from the beginning was not just to start another church. I truly believed at that time and still do that God had called us for so much more than just filling seats. As the years have passed, what I have found out is that God's plans are so much greater than my plans. The truth is that His plans are even better than my plans.

As followers of Jesus, sometimes we make plans and then ask God to join us in them. When the truth is that God already has a plan and He wants us to join Him in that plan. The even better news is that His plan is so much better and greater than our plan.

THE BIG FOUR

As I sat there in the "Global Leadership Summit" put on by Willow Creek Association and thought about the way this summit was reaching thousands of people at one time through simulcasting, I realized that God really wanted to ramp things up in my life and the life of The Vertical Church. We had reached a milestone at The Vertical Church. We were averaging a little over 200 people and were setting comfortable. I was 35 years old and had been at this planting/pastoring thing for a while now.

It was in that moment that Jesus was asking me to take a risk again. You see Jesus always calls us in the moment of our comfort. He says, "You're comfortable, I have a plan, will you step out of your comfort and join me?"

I opened my iPad and begin typing what I call now, "The Big Four." I figured I had about 30 more good years to serve The Vertical Church at a high capacity. As the conference went on, I began to ask God, "How do you want me to spend the next 30 years?" God began to speak to me with spontaneous thoughts and I began to write them down. Here is what came out of that crisis of belief. Jesus was asking The Vertical Church to partner with Him and Risk Crazy in the next 30 years by:

1. Seeing 10,000 people come to know Him through our services.
2. Help the Helpless: This meaning to partner, empower, and help those without a voice. We consider the children ones who have no voice.
3. Empower The Poor
4. Help Plant 100 Churches in the United States.

When we began The Vertical Church in 2005, I never dreamed that Jesus would ask us to partner with Him to do these things above. I realized in that moment that Jesus was asking us to step out in faith at a level that I was not familiar with. This was way beyond what we could ever think or imagine on our own.

When you partner with Jesus to make a change in this world, He will open doors for you to walk through and follow Him. As you do this, it will empower others to do the same as well as blow your mind thinking about what He is asking of you!

Of course, this was only a document on my iPad. I knew I had to tell someone. Then I had to eventually share this with our congregation. What would people think? How would people respond? It sounds so huge, how can a 200-person church in Yuma, Arizona do anything of any significance; much less fulfill these lofty goals? Remember that verse you just read, Ephesians 3:20-21? It said, *"Now to him who is able to do immeasurable more than all we ask or imagine..."* I knew that, I believed that, but how? I read a quote by Barry St. Clair years ago that said this, "Vision is something that is so great that unless God does it you're doomed to failure." After writing down what I believed Jesus was asking, I felt the heaviness of the matter but knew that God had to do it or it would fail.

That was August. Over the course of the next couple of months, I had smaller meetings of influential people in our church. I shared what Jesus was asking us to do. To my surprise, not one person pushed back. Maybe they were used to this risking crazy message, or maybe they were empowered by seeing Jesus move in our midst over the last few years; either way, I was happy that they all received it with open hearts. But the day was coming when I would have to announce this to our church.

On that fateful Sunday, I started a series called, "Full Throttle." I talked about what I just shared with you in how Jesus was asking us to commit the next 30 years to fulfilling these goals.

65

I talked about how that we have been coasting as a church and we need to get into first gear.

You do know that first gear is the hardest gear to get into when driving a stick shift vehicle. I remember when my dad was teaching me to drive my first car, which was a stick shift. He had me practice repeatedly, on a hillside, rolling backwards and then getting the car to go into first gear. I practiced and practiced and killed the engine so many times, I thought I would never get it. Finally, out of nowhere, I got it. Then I got it again, and again. I had this thing.

What I realized was getting into first gear without killing the engine was the hardest part. After that, the other gears shifted smoothly. In our lives, we tend to coast a lot. The problem with coasting is you encounter hills, upward and downward. Coasting is fun when you are going downhill. It is when you stop at the bottom of the hill or when you are approaching the bottom of another hill, it quickly becomes no fun at all. The truth is that you have to have some outside force to push your vehicle along. Either you have to learn how to drive on your own, or you have to rely on someone to push you.

I explained to the church that we have had people pushing us for a while. We had had awesome supporters financially give to help start The Vertical Church. But somewhere along the way, we have to stop coasting and we have to get rolling on our own. This was our first gear. And, it was going to be the hardest.

That day, people committed to give financially above and beyond what they normally give for the next 12 months to hit our "First Gear Goals."

People were excited! But over that three week series, our attendance started to really drop. It scared me! As a person who planted a church, you have this continual fear of showing up to church one Sunday and nobody will be there. Why? Because you remember the days when nobody showed up.

I kept clinging to that verse—"more than we could ever think or imagine." He was going to do something great. The Apostle Paul wrote in Ephesians 3:20-21 a great ending to a great prayer for this church in Ephesus. But the prayer started a few verses earlier. In fact, he said this:

"I pray that out of his glorious riches he may strengthen you with power through his Spirit in your inner being" (Ephesians 3:16).

The strength to "follow Him" does not come from your repeated good actions. It does not come from you mustering up enough courage to push beyond the limits you have on yourself. It is not about good self-esteem. No. Jesus works when we are at our weakest. He works within us through His spiritual power to transform our lives and use us to transform lives around us.

It is scary to follow Jesus. If you are going to commit to this risking crazy lifestyle and take risks—that some might call crazy—for Jesus, you will face your greatest fears. My greatest fear was messing up this whole church planting/pastoring thing. I was facing it head on. Our church had grown, we were comfortable, and now God was decreasing the size of our church. Why God? I thought you called me to this. I thought you said to do this. What are you doing God?

GOD'S MATH IS DIFFERENT THAN OUR MATH

What I didn't know then, but do now is that God's math is different ours. Is that not what He even says in His word about "His ways": "For my thoughts are not your thoughts, neither are your ways my ways,' declares the Lord. As the heavens are higher than the earth, so are my ways higher than your ways and my thoughts than your thoughts" (Isaiah 55:8-9).

The ways of the Lord are so drastically different from ours. Think about it. Who dies for a person who is so sinful and unrighteous? Jesus does. No one else does. Who gives mercy and grace when we deserve death and damnation? Jesus does. No one else does that. His ways are different. And His math is different.

God always knows what He is doing. Nothing ever surprises Him. It is not as if God is up and heaven and looks down and says, "WOW! That one caught me by surprise! I didn't see that coming." He knew the moment He asked me to step out and take a risk with this long-term vision that people would leave. He knew I would face this fear again. He was doing a work in me.

A few months after the series ended, God began to add more people and finances to carry out the future vision. We were getting into "First Gear" as a church. As I look back, I see it as an exciting but scary time where God grew all of our faith. Before I go on, let me tell you how we are doing so far in this vision.

As I am writing this, I am 38 years old. So in the last 3 years since the announcement of that vision, we have grown by over 400 extra people in average attendance. God's math is different than ours. Since then a little over 700 people have given their lives to Jesus through our services and we have baptized close to 400. As Paul wrote in Ephesians 3:21, "to him be glory in the church and in Christ Jesus.". A year after that series, we sent our first church planter from our church to Michigan to start a new church. Less than a year later, we sent some of our people along with another church planter to plant a new church in Yuma. This feeds into the goal of seeing 100 churches planted in the United States in 30 years.

By God's grace, we were connected with a program called "PowerPack" which helps feed kids on the weekends who rely on the free school lunch program in our city. We are partnering with two schools in our community and other churches are jumping in to help as well. This is part of the goal of "Helping the Helpless."

As for "Empowering the Poor," we have started partnering with a pastor about 30 miles from us in Mexico who is starting churches, building clinics for the poor, and help start a crisis pregnancy center for young ladies needing help.

This is just the beginning. The best is yet to come. How do I know? Because God says He can do more than we can ever think or imagine.

As you follow Him in this lifestyle of taking risks, He will do a work in you. In fact, He will work on you before He works through you. You and I have no power of our own to do what Jesus asks. What Paul wrote to that church in Ephesus is for us today as well. Our only power comes from His Spirit in our "inner being." He gives you strength in your "inner being" to carry out what He is asking you to do.

The Apostle Paul goes on to write: "So that Christ may dwell in your hearts through faith. And I pray that you, being rooted and established in love, may have power, together with all the Lord's holy people, to grasp how wide and long and high and deep is the love of Christ, and to know this love that surpasses knowledge—that you may be filled to the measure of all the fullness of God" (Ephesians 3:17-19).

Paul is praying for Christ to be so established in our hearts that we will be able to comprehend a love that surpasses anything we know. As we dwell on the love that Jesus has for us, we will have no problem risking crazy and following Him no matter where He leads us.

The first three chapters of Ephesians are about Paul making a case for how that when we are in Christ we are made alive from our deadness, not because of anything we have done, but because of His great love. He continues in chapter four to talk about the body that is being built up called "The Church." He even says in 3:18: "together with all the Lord's holy people," implying that we are all in this thing together.

There are people all over the world who have placed their faith in Jesus Christ and He is continually calling them to step out of their comfort just like He is you. All of us together "being rooted in this love" can change the world around us. We can make a difference that will make eternal impact. You can be a part of something bigger than you, by following Him. I believe that He calls us along life's path to risk crazy at a deeper level. It is no longer about just building buildings and filling buildings. It is about the church being the hands and feet of Jesus to a dying world. As we do this, they see the kindness of God and then turn to the gospel of Jesus Christ.

But it takes millions of people who say they are following Jesus to actually follow Him. It takes us not being afraid of taking a step of faith even though those around us call us crazy. Paul goes on to write in chapter four of Ephesians: "As a prisoner for the Lord, then, I urge you to live a life worthy of the calling you have received" (Ephesians 4:1).

Paul is reminding us that we are "prisoners" for the Lord. We are now slaves to His righteousness and grace. Because of that, we can through His power, live the life He has called us to. He goes on to say, "Be completely humble and gentle; be patient, bearing with one another in love. Make every effort to keep the unity of the Spirit through the bond of peace" (Ephesians 4:2-3).

The only way we can carry out these attitudes of humbleness, gentleness, and patience is through the grace that Jesus has given us. It is through that grace that we can now carry out good works. Paul is building up to the proclamation that there is "one body," called the Church, in this world carrying out the call of Jesus. What is it that unifies us? It is the "bond of peace." This peace is outside of us. It is a peace we have with God. We are no longer at war with God because of our sin, but now have peace through His Son, Jesus. This is the unifying factor.

Again, Paul is building up to let us in on the glorious body that Jesus is calling to follow Him together to be His hands and feet in this world. Continuing he writes in verse 11: "So Christ himself gave the apostles, the prophets, the evangelists, the pastors and teachers, to equip his people for works of service, so that the body of Christ may be built up until we all reach full unity in the faith and in the knowledge of the Son of God and become mature, attaining the whole measure of the fullness of Christ" (Ephesians 4:11-13).

He is saying that Jesus gave preachers, teachers, prophets, and evangelists gifts to carry out His work in the church. So many of us lay all of the ministering upon the "paid professionals." I do not know who that is in your context. Maybe it is a pastor, or a missionary, or some other paid staff at your church. The truth is that according to this passage, Jesus gave these people, the paid staff at your church, for one reason: To equip you to do the work of ministry.

Now that is a paradigm shift in your mind. I truly believe that the greatest ministry that takes place in The Vertical Church or any church is not from the pastor but from the people in the seats who decide to start risking crazy for Jesus. Why did Jesus do that? Paul says, "so that the body of Christ may be built up." The only way for the church to be the church is not through "paid professionals." It is done by each of us deciding to follow Jesus daily.

Maturing in Christ is not about how much Bible you read or know. Sure, that is a great thing. It is not becoming a "paid professional" at the church. Sure, there is a need for that. It is finding your place in this glorious body called the Church. It is about finding how your preacher/teacher has equipped you for the work of the ministry. It is about you letting the power of Christ in your inner being, be the fuel that gets you into "first gear" and on to the "full throttle" lifestyle. It is about stopping the "coast." It is about taking this risking crazy lifestyle to another level.

NEXT STEPS

1. What are some larger than life tasks that you see happening in the worldwide church of Jesus Christ?
2. When you hear about these great stories of faith, what feelings rise inside of you?
3. What are some ways you can partner with what God is already doing in your community, church, or the worldwide church to take risking crazy to another level?
4. What are some ways that God has gifted you through the Spirit to "do the work of the ministry"?
5. Is there anything that the "paid professional" at your church is doing that you he/she could equip you to do?
6. Write down some ways you are going to step up in the "body of Christ" and risk crazy.

CHAPTER 10

KINDNESS IN PROGRESS

As a child growing up in church, we used to sing a song called, "He's Still Working On Me." The truth is that at the moment of salvation, we are forgiven of all our sins. However, there is a work in progress going on until the day we stand glorified in Him in heaven. The work for our salvation was already done on the cross of Jesus. We are now supposed to be living under the banner of "It is finished" while preaching the gospel of grace to ourselves every day.

We do good works and risk crazy to glorify the Father in heaven because we are already blessed and full of grace. Jesus said it this way in the Sermon on The Mount: "In the same way, let your light shine before others, that they may see your good deeds and glorify your Father in heaven" (Matthew 5:16).

It takes risk to perform good deeds. It may not seem like a risk when you are showing kindness to a random stranger; however, every selfish desire within you rises up to fight your effort the moment you surrender and say you will follow what God is asking. In those moments, we can remember we have a Father in heaven who gives us the power to take risks to see Him glorified unconditionally loves us.

The struggle is for a lifetime. As soon as you step out in faith, doubt will come, your faith will be challenged, and others might even ridicule you. We will be tempted to falter in our resolve.

You might even consider, is it worth it? We will be tempted not to believe that God is who He says He is or that He can do what He says He can do. Can I tell you to just relax? This is part of the risking crazy lifestyle. This is kindness in progress.

RELAX

What God may be asking you to do, may feel a bit overwhelming. That is understandable. I have struggled with feeling inadequate, unequipped, and unworthy to do the things that He has asked me to do. Sometimes we can really beat ourselves up because we live in a performance-based world.

In fact you may start to feel as if God is in heaven judging you based on your performance. Maybe you feel as if you are constantly under a performance review by the Heavenly Father. Sometimes we even do good works out of guilt. We feel an overwhelming sense of guilt because of all the need and we must do something. Let me just repeat: Relax!

I asked my kids the other day a very important question: "What do you think God thinks of you?" I asked them at separate times apart from each other because I did not want their answers to be influence by one another. My daughter quickly said, "He thinks I'm AWESOME!" She said it with a HUGE smile on her face. She did not even stop to think about it. It was amazing. I quickly agreed with her.

The truth is that if you are a believer in God's Son, Jesus Christ, for your salvation, God does think you're awesome. Before you ever do any good deed. Before you ever step out in faith and follow Him. Before you ever find a need and fill it. God thinks you're awesome.

Here's why: At the moment of salvation, you become the righteousness of God in Christ Jesus. Which means when God looks at you, He no longer sees your sin but the righteousness of His Son, Jesus! At that moment, you are justified. Justification is what takes place when God forgives you of all of your sin. It is living under the banner of "It Is Finished." You are at that moment saved. This is the beginning of following Christ with your life.

As you continue in this walk with Jesus, you start the process of sanctification. This is simply becoming more like Jesus. You and I both know we will never become perfect, as Jesus is perfect. This is why we have trusted in His perfection and substitution for the payment of our sins. Risking Crazy is about the sanctification process that does not end until our earthly lives end.

During this sanctifying craziness, we find needs and ask God to help us fill that need not to gain a higher standing with God, but to glorify Him while being the hands and feet of Jesus to those without faith. You are not only saved at the moment of salvation, but are now being saved during your lifetime. While all of this is going on, God thinks you're awesome!

One day will come when we will breathe our last breath. We will stand before the holy God of the universe. God will look back over our life and will remember the time we placed our faith in Jesus. He will know that we are justified through His Son and are saved. He will look at our good works and reward us for them knowing that we were doing the best we could to become more like His Son. At that moment, our bodies will be glorified. Simply meaning that there will be no more sin. There will be no more struggle, there will be no more need to risk crazy.

So relax! Live in the daily dependence of the Holy Spirit guiding you step out, and follow Him. This lifestyle is not about burdens. It is simply about living in the truth that God thinks you're awesome. It is about resting in the truth that "It Is Finished."

REST

Over the years as a pastor, my struggle has been rest. No, not sleep. I can sleep just fine. But simply rest. I try to make things happen. I try to live outside of my comfort to the point of slipping into the legalism of thinking God is not pleased with me. I struggle every day to live under "It Is Finished" instead of your performance equals God's love for you.

I have lived my life at break neck speeds at times thinking that I was somehow pleasing God more because I was doing more. When in reality my soul was dying. You ever been there? Maybe you realize that you are in this spot now. Maybe you are feeling restlessness instead of rest. Let me encourage you with the words of Jesus: "Come to me, all you who are weary and burdened, and I will give you rest. Take my yoke upon you and learn from me, for I am gentle and humble in heart, and you will find rest for your souls. For my yoke is easy and my burden is light" (Matthew 11:28-30).

About four years into this church plant, I felt a heavy burden from God to spend more time with Him in prayer. I read about people in history who would rise early and pray for hours. I begin to ask the question "Why can't I rise early and pray for at least one hour?" So I made a commitment to do just that.

That first morning was epic. I had never experienced anything like sitting in the presence of God for one uninterrupted hour and communing with Him. I got to where I even planned on going to bed early at night because I did not want to miss this awesome time with God. It was during that time that I felt a closeness like never before. I did this for several months. Then something changed.

Somewhere along the way, the point of this time with God changed from spending time with Him to how much time am I spending. I began keeping track of my time spent with God.

What I am about to tell you sounds completely ridiculous. I literally was keeping a time clock and a tally sheet on how many hours I would spend with God. Then I made it a competition with myself. I thought to myself, "Why not two hours?" So I made that commitment and set the goal.

You see what I was doing was turning this relationship into a legalistic religion. Jesus never intended for His yoke to be hard and burdensome. He said it is "easy." At the time that our church was growing tremendously, we were risking crazy like never before, and I was communing with God for hours each day. Then I hit the wall.

I really cannot explain exactly what that wall was. All I know is that time with God became burdensome. There were days that I did not make the two hours and I would beat myself up and think that God was mad at me. I literally thought God must have been punishing me because something bad would happen on those days.

It became hard to get to sleep at night. Anxiety went through the roof. I did not want to be around people. All I wanted to do was to go to my bedroom, turn out the lights, draw the curtains, and sleep. But even that brought no relief from the darkness of the soul I was experiencing. I remember sitting at our local Starbucks across the table from a pastor friend of mine in Yuma with tears streaming down my face feeling like a complete failure, yet our church was growing and reaching more people than ever before. The hours I spent with God turned into minutes.

I had heard people use a word before about what was happening: burnout. But the truth is I never thought it would happen to me. I thought, "Those people were weak, I'm not weak! I spend an hour a day with God in prayer!" But it was happening. By God's grace, I did not completely burn out.

From the advice of this trusted friend, I made an appointment with my doctor. She immediately put me on antidepressants. Which made things worse for me. So I quickly came off of those. She referred me to a Counselor. He worked in with her to provide the counseling side of things while recommending medications. I went through several. While this was going on, I found a Christian Counselor and started to meet with him at the same time. Through all of that combination of non-Christian counseling, Christian Counseling, and medicine, I realized that I needed a HUGE lifestyle change that involved rest.

But there was a problem. I could not just quit everything I was doing. One counselor said, "If you stopped for 3-6 months, you could possibly recover." I told him that was not an option. Then he explained to me how I needed to change my eating habits, exercise routine, and schedule to be able to have some sort of recovery over the next 9 months. So that is what I did. What I needed was rest while still being engaged in real life.

Now let me stop right here. I want you to understand that I know that some people need to just stop and rest. They cannot just make a few adjustments here and there. They cannot just go off the medication. For some people, they may need to stop everything and rest. But for me, a lifestyle change was what helped me. I had to conclude that living a life of following hard after Jesus is not a burdensome task. That Jesus is tapping me on the shoulder, but He does not expect me to be the Savior of the world. He is. Following Him is about coming to Him and finding rest. Denying yourself, taking up your cross, and following Him is bathed in rest. I truly believe you can do both.

Rest is risk. You have to trust that God will take care of the needs even after you have exhausted all of your resources. You have to trust that you are following Him the best you know how and He is not up in heaven mad or angry with you because you did not save the world. It is not your job to save the world. It is your job just simply to follow the leading of His Spirit while resting in the truth that His payment on the cross has finished the work for you. The risk factor comes in the trust. Fully trusting that God will let His will play out even in spite of you.

It is great to know that God chooses to partner with people to carry out His will. It is great to feel like you are part of helping change the world. But at the end of the day, God is in control and there is nothing you can do to change that.

You may be thinking, "So Jason, do you still pray and read your Bible?" Yes, I just don't count the minutes anymore or the chapters read. I simply rest in Him. I no longer believe that every bad thing that happens to me is because I did not follow through with something He asked of me. I rest in the fact that I can never be more saved than I am now. I am the righteousness of God in Christ Jesus.

The problem with us humans is that we turn everything into religion. It is as if we really do not believe that Jesus has taken care of all our sins. We live as if it is not finished. In reality, you can do nothing to add to your salvation. The reason we reach out in kindness and follow Jesus in faith risks is not to get more blessing, but to live out the blessings with which He has already blessed us.

Jesus said, "His yoke is easy and my burden is light." This means the very thing that He is asking you to do may seem hard in your mind, but in Him, it is easy. I know it may sound like I am contradicting myself right now, but I want you to understand that the work of following the leading or Jesus in your life is about doing it with the attitude of rest. You and I are a work in progress. . It is life-long. He is still working on you.

RENEW

The life we are living through Jesus Christ is in progress. We are changing by the minute to become more like Him. We can rest knowing that whatever He asks of us, He will accomplish it in His time. But at the same time, I believe Jesus calls us, as we follow Him, to be renewed.

When you place your faith in Jesus, you are a new creation. The old is gone. The new has come. Paul said in Romans: "Therefore, I urge you, brothers and sisters, in view of God's mercy, to offer your bodies as living sacrifice, holy and pleasing to God—this is your true and proper worship. Do not conform to the pattern of this world, but be transformed by the renewing of your mind. Then you will be able to test and approve what God's will is—his good, pleasing and perfect will" (Romans 12:1-2).

Paul has given you and I a charge to be that "living sacrifice." This will take a surrender of your will. When you lay your life down on the altar of surrender, you are denying yourself and becoming a living sacrifice. You are not dead, but have died to yourself and are now living for the glory of Jesus.

What causes us to be able to do this? It is not because we are inherently good people. It is not because we just simply see a need and want to meet that need. No, Paul tells us in verse one: "...in view of God's mercy." In other words, because of this great grace and mercy that God has shown to us, we can now freely offer our bodies as "living sacrifices." We can take those risks—that some might call crazy—for Jesus.

Chapter 12 of Romans is one of the turning points in the book. Up to this point in this book, Paul has reminded us of our sin, and then our need for a Savior. At this stage, he turns the attention to how we should then live out this grace life God has called and saved us to. So he says...

"Do not conform to the pattern of this world."

Because of all that was said in chapters 1-11, Paul can now tell us how to live. Because of God's mercy, we now have the power not to "conform." Conformity would be to believe that your righteous acts are what bring God's goodness to your life.

When in reality in Jesus, we are already blessed. Our righteous acts bring glory to the Father and help us to be the hands and feet of Jesus to others. Conforming is staying with the status quo. Conforming is just going to church. Conforming believes that life is all about me. Conforming is not being willing to deny yourself, take up your cross, and follow Jesus wherever He leads. Because of the great mercy of God, we do not have to conform.

"...but be transformed..."

Jesus lived, died, and rose from the grave so we do not have to "conform" but we can be "transformed." Our lives are changed. We are no longer the same. In Christ, you are now the righteousness of God. In the same way, we have the power now to see other people's lives transformed because of the great mercy and grace flowing from God, out of us, and onto others. Because of that great promise, we can now live out the life for which Jesus has called us. We are not to conform but be transformed. How?

"...by the renewing of your mind..."

Paul exhorts us not to conform, but be transformed, and then tells us how. We are to renew our mind. As you relax in God's grace and rest in His perfect plan. You will then be able to truly live out this passage and have a mind renewal that permeates all of who you are. If we jump right into the renewing, I believe we will end up burning out or flaming out. We will come to the place where it is all based on our works and not by the grace by which we are saved. The renewal is a transition of the mind that takes place. It is the transition from, "The pressure is all on me to perform" to "God is in complete control." This renewal happens when the foundation is built on relaxing and resting. The final sentence sums it up:

"Then you will be able to test and approve what God's will is—his good, pleasing and perfect will."

What is God's will for my life? What is His plan? Am I following Jesus and denying myself? Have I taken up my cross? Have I truly lived a life that is full of risks for the glory of Jesus? The only way to know is by relaxing, resting, and then renewing the mind to the point of accepting that my life is kindness in progress. The next verse Paul says this: "For by the grace given me I say to every one of you: Do not think of yourself more highly than you ought, but rather think of yourself with sober judgment, in accordance with the faith God has distributed to each of you" (Romans 12:3).

How do we view ourselves? The view we have of ourselves will determine how we treat others. Paul switches gears in this chapter and begins to talk about how the church is the body of Christ and we all work together with differing gifts to carry out His plan for the world. Each believer has been created by God and been given grace to be able to take risks—that some might call crazy—for Jesus. Paul says not to think too highly of yourself. As we work together as the body of Christ, we can truly make kingdom impact for His glory.

Our lives are kindness in progress. We are on this path to stand before a holy God. The only hope we have is in Jesus. He justifies us, sanctifies us, and then later glorifies our bodies in heaven. Remember, He is still working on you. So relax, rest, and renew.

NEXT STEPS

1. When looking at the bigger picture of your life, how would you describe your spiritual progress?
2. Why do we find it so difficult to believe that in Jesus we truly are forgiven and free?

3. In what ways does your life need to change to reflect the promise that "It is finished"?
4. What needs to change in your life to find rest for your soul while still taking risks for Jesus?
5. Take a day and set aside time to reflect on the promises of God, pray, rest, and renew your mind.
6. Which word, relax, rest, or renew is God asking you to focus on right now?

CHAPTER 11

LIVING A LIFE OF RISK

What if? Have you ever thought that? I believe that Jesus has called us to live life to the fullest. Through His power, we can do that. I do not believe for one second that Jesus wants us to leave "what ifs" on the table of our life. He wants us to jump full force and risk crazy for Him.

While Melissa and I were dating, we took a youth group to Fort Worth, Texas for a denominational convention. This trip was the first real youth trip as a brand new youth pastor still in college. At the end of the convention, we took the youth group to Six Flags. We rode the rides with enthusiasm and had a great experience. Toward the end of the day, we noticed a ride called "The Skycoaster." The students with us on this trip challenged Melissa and I to ride this giant free fall bungee cord ride that would fling us many stories up into the sky.

Being young and adventurous, we decided that this was a once in a lifetime chance. I still remember the sheer terror on Melissa's face as they strapped us into this harness to hold our bodies side by side together. Then they tethered us onto this giant bungee rope. They told us while on the ground that we would hear someone say over a speaker, "3-2-1" and at that point, one of us was to pull the ripcord to release us from the safety of the top of this giant arch.

As the machine was lifting us facedown into the air, we both started to rethink this decision. Then we were locked into place. On the way up, Melissa decided that I was to be the one to pull the cord. The man came on the speaker, "3-2-1" and I reached back and pulled the cord.

We were then flung into a free fall for about 5 seconds until the cord reached its full length and then swung us through the arch like a giant pendulum back and forth for a few more minutes. We were literally soaring like a bird back and forth. It was one of the most exhilarating moments of our lives.

Living a life of risk is just like that ride. First, you have to make a decision that you are going to take on this lifestyle with no holds barred. The truth is that when you put your faith in Jesus, you have then said, "Yes" not to just salvation, but for whatever adventure that might hold. He straps you into the salvation harness that is completely safe and secure.

By His power, He pulls you back and up into the sky. He is getting you ready for the ride ahead. For some of us that pull backward is a long ride. Sometimes God has to prepare us for what is about to come. On the way up and back, we wrestle with these questions of faith:

What if this does not work out?
What if I mess up?
What if I completely fail?
What if...?

At this point, we must decide. Are we going to pull the ripcord? When God says, "3-2-1," what will we do? It is in these moments that we decide to live a life of risk.

What if I pull the cord? Maybe a better question to ask is, "What if I do not pull the cord?" Whose life might not be changed? What cause will go unmet? What person in my life will not experience this ride that I am about to experience? What if I don't pull the cord? What will not happen?

God is asking you to pull that cord. He will not pull it for you. Melissa and I would have not dropped into that free fall and then into the glorious ride until we pulled that cord. I look back on the lives that have been changed so far through risk and faith and God's power, I praise Him that He allowed us to pull that cord on the ride and the life of risk.

FREE FALLING

I have to be honest. That ride is a picture of the life of risk. The free fall that occurred immediately after pulling the cord resembles the free fall that happens when you pull the cord on your life of risk. When you choose to take risks—that some might call crazy—for Jesus, that first pull of the cord will result in a free fall. I can look back over my life and see free fall after free fall. But every time the ride smoothed out and the ride has been worth the initial frightening free fall.

We do not have all the answers. We do not know the future. But Jesus is calling you and I to risk without knowing all of that. Jesus does. And that is all we need. We can trust that the free fall may feel frightening, but we are still strapped into His harness and tied to the power rope of the Holy Spirit. As you step out in faith and do things you never thought possible, the ride will be worth the free fall. Just take the next step in front of you and pull that cord.

LISTEN TO EVERY MOMENT

I wish I could write about your life personally and tell you exactly what Jesus is asking of you. But I cannot. I am not God. All I can say is to commit to being a person who listens. Living a life of risk is about listening for the voice of the Spirit in you.

By now, I trust you have been practicing this. Living a life of risk is about listening to every moment in front of you. Begin to ask these questions:

What is God saying in this moment?

Remember He is always speaking. I have set in situations and simply said, "God speak to me in this moment." You will be amazed at what you will hear as you practice this discipline.

Who is with me in this moment that I need to ask to join me?

God is always raising up an army. You can be sure that if He has spoken to you about something, He has also called others to join you in that endeavor. Who are those people? Maybe you are in a small group at your church and you have felt the voice of God move you in a direction. Why not share that with your group? Then ask, "Is there anyone who would like to join me?" Do not get mad if no one speaks up. Give it some time. Even if no one joins you, you need to answer the next question.

How is this endeavor growing the kingdom of God?

The kingdom of God is much bigger than one church, denomination, or group. It is much larger than a local body of believers. But it is within the local church that it begins. As you get others on board, cast a vision for influencing the world and growing the kingdom. There is no doubt within the worldwide body of Christ there is someone with a similar vision that you have. You can join up with them and affect more people. What if churches could gather around a common cause in a singular city? I realize we all worship differently and have some minor belief differences; but what would it look like if the body of Christ in one region or city decided to tackle a cause. That is risk. That is kingdom impact. But, someone has to pull the cord. That someone is you.

STEP OUT IN FAITH

Faith is so powerful. I have seen God move mightily because of His will and glory and our faith. Living a life of risk is about stepping out in faith, not just once, or twice, but repeatedly. The writer of Hebrews said this: "Now faith is confidence of what we hope for and assurance about what we do not see" (Hebrews 11:1).

You will not know the outcome. God does. You have to live a life that trusts that He knows the outcome and has His glory in mind. Faith is confidence. It is seeing a picture of the future that God gives you and seeing it through to completion. But you have to step out in faith. One of my favorite songs, "Voice of Truth," is by a band named, Casting Crowns. I would encourage you to listen to the song.

This song tells us not to listen to the voices around us or even in us, but to the one voice that is truth—His name is Jesus. Risking Crazy is about taking risks—that some might call crazy—for Jesus. When you step out in faith, you will be called crazy. But that is part of the process. That is part of the risking crazy lifestyle.

YOUR JOURNEY HAS JUST STARTED

Only Jesus knows the ending. If someone would have told me at 15 years of age that saying "Yes" to Jesus' call on my life would have led me to Yuma, Arizona to start a church, I would have laughed my head off. I could have never dreamed up on my own the journey that God has been taking me on. This I do know. He is not finished with me. Nor is He finished with you.

You may feel like what I am talking about is just too overwhelming. Maybe you think that it is okay for me or for your pastor, but not for you. The truth is that He is calling men and women everywhere to change the world. He is tapping you on

89

the shoulder and asking you to follow Him. Will you respond with a "Yes"? Will you deny yourself, take up your cross, and follow Him? Will you let Him write the journey and trust Him along the way? These are questions you must wrestle with. These are thoughts that you have to reconcile in your own soul. But this I do know. He is calling. He is working around you. Will you find out where that is and join Him?

One of my life verses is this: "Being confident of this, that he who began a good work in you will carry it on to completion until the day of Christ Jesus" (Philippians 1:6). When I read that verse, which I have many times, I think of my life. I think of what He has asked of me and is continually asking and remember that He is not done with me. That my journey is just beginning. Yours is too.

He Began the Work

You did not start this. He did. You did not choose Him as much as He has chosen you. He has begun the work. If He has begun the work, then you can have confidence. You can know that it is for His glory and by His power that it started. If He has begun the work, then He has a plan. If He has a plan, you can trust the outcome.

It Is a Good Work

The verse goes on to tell us that it is not just any work. It is a "good work." You might be able to add that it is a "good" and glorious work. No matter what you think of the outcome, the work is good. If God calls it good, then it is good.

The Work Started in You

The next part of that verse says "in you." The work was started in you. This tells us of the uniqueness of His calling. Just because God called me to preach and then start a church does not

90

mean that calling is for everyone. Yes, there are some universal callings such as "going and making disciples" and "loving your neighbor as yourself"; however, He has a unique plan for you. The work started uniquely in you for your city and through your church. This gets my blood pumping to think that the God of the universe cared enough to include me in His overall plan in a unique way.

He Will Carry It

As you continue reading the passage, you see that God is the carrier of this "good work." This takes a lot of pressure off us. This gives us the freedom to rest, relax, and renew while following Him. He carries it.

He Will Complete It

Sometimes I lay awake at night wondering about the future. But this verse tells me that I should just go to sleep because He is the one who will complete the work in me. Paul is writing to this church thanking them and telling them of how he is praying for them. They have been partners in the gospel. At the time, Paul is imprisoned for the faith. He is reassuring them that the partnering work that began in them will be completed. He is putting all his confidence in Jesus. He is the one who will complete it.

Our Work Is Complete When Jesus Returns

I believe this is tied to the second return of Jesus. The early church lived as if Jesus was returning sometime that day. We have seen thousands of years pass, but when Paul wrote this, he was referring to the return of Jesus. Implying that our work is not done until Jesus returns. The phrase "the day" tells us that there will come a day when there will be no more poverty, tears, sin, or even a reason to evangelize. Our work is not complete until "the day."

Obviously, we have no idea when that is. In the meantime, He is calling us to live the risking crazy lifestyle everyday as if today is "the day." Paul repeats this theme later in the passage when he says: "And this is my prayer: that your love may abound more and more in knowledge and depth of insight, so that you may be able to discern what is best and may be pure and blameless for the day of Christ, filled with the fruit of righteousness that comes through Jesus Christ—to the glory and praise of God" (Philippians 1:9-11).

What is his ultimate prayer for this church? That their love may abound more and more. Paul said on another occasion in 1 Corinthians 13:13, "And now these three remain: faith, hope and love. But the greatest of these is love."

Chapter 13 of 1 Corinthians is in the middle of Paul's address of this church's disagreement on the use of spiritual gifts. He tells us in this chapter that no matter how great the gifting, if there is not love, it is useless.

We see the theme repeated in Philippians as Paul says his prayer is that their love may abound more and more. Love is a big issue. When it comes to living the risking crazy lifestyle, we must determine our motivating factor. Love must be it. If it is not love, then we are fulfilling our own selfish desires. The desire to change the world, if left unchecked, can be motivated by our own desire to build a name for our self. But love washes that goal away. When love is our motivating factor, then it all changes.

I am not just talking about any kind of love but a love that is for God first, then others. It is the kind of love that Jesus taught us about in the New Testament. It is the kind of servant leadership type love. When our love for God becomes greater than our love for self, then our natural outflow will be a love for others.

So as you walk in this risking crazy lifestyle, determine that love will be the motivating factor. And remember that the work is not up to you to complete. He is in complete control.

WHERE DO I GO FROM HERE?

In life, there have been times where I have been motivated and inspired to do great things but walked away with an overwhelming feeling that I could not accomplish it. Why? I did not know where to start. We have talked about denying yourself, taking up your cross, and following Him. We have talked about surrender and faith and starting small. We have covered the truth that Jesus is in complete control; however, at the end of the day, you have to get up from your current status quo and rise to the risking crazy lifestyle. But, where do you start. Here is a question to start with:

What Will My Life Look Like In 30 Years?

This can be a penetrating question. Now I am assuming by now that you are surrendered to this risking crazy lifestyle. You have said, no matter what, I am going to do what Jesus asks of me even if some might call it crazy. So as we move past all of that, what will my life look like in 30 years?

Thirty years is a long time. There is a reason I chose that number. Here's why. No matter how old you are when you read this, you can make a significant difference in 30 years. The truth is that none of us can predict the future. We cannot truthfully see what the next 30 years will hold. However, we can determine some of the general priorities that we will focus on. We can determine whom we will live for. We can determine some core values in our life. We can figure out how we will live out those values. We also can determine how we will not live out those values. With that said, would you stop and consider what the next 30 years will look like for you. But before you start drawing a picture of that, let's start with prayer.

START WITH PRAYER

Throughout this book, I have emphasized prayer. I do not want to end this book without reorienting you to this idea of prayer as the catalyst for any change in your life and others. The faith filled life starts with a prayer of surrender. There is ongoing prayer throughout your life. There is self-denying prayer that takes place on a moment-by-moment basis. And it is through prayer that Jesus speaks to us. So as you think about your next 30 years, start with prayer. Here are some ideas to remember when praying:

Surrender Your Future To Him

Give Jesus your future. The Risking Crazy prayer at the end of chapter one said this: Father, I come to You because of what Jesus accomplished for me through His death and resurrection. I confess to You my attitudes of selfishness, love of comfort, and greed. Please make my life—my desires, my perspectives—what You want, what You desire. I want to say yes to Your plans. Amen.

You might want to add something like this: Father, I give You my future. As I think about the next 30 years, give me Your thoughts not mine.

This posture of praying leads into a life of surrender. The lifestyle of following Jesus begins with surrender and continues with surrender. Sometimes we are afraid of what Jesus might ask of us. However, the truth is that no matter what it is, we will be able to accomplish it through His power. Now 30 years is a long time. So do not expect God to give you every little detail for the next 30 years in one setting. I would say that He will not reveal any real details to you. If we had all the details, why would we need God? He is going to move on your heart to align your values with His.

Ask God for the Impossible

As your posture continues in that of surrender, take time to ask God to help you be involved with what others might think impossible. Apply your faith to your prayers and ask Him for great things. Maybe in these moments, you do not know exactly what to ask. So I would suggest you pray prayers of faith in whom He is. In other words, acknowledge that He can do the impossible. Through your prayers, let Him know that you truly believe He will accomplish His will through you. Let him know clearly that you are on board no matter what. You will be surprised at how these faith-building prayers will open your eyes to the needs around you.

Ask Him to Open Your Eyes to the Needs Around You

As you apply your faith to these prayers, ask God to open your eyes. We walk by people every day who need Jesus. We rub shoulders with people who have little or no hope in their life. Ask the God of the universe to open your eyes to those people and their needs. Make this an ongoing prayer. As you live each day, before your feet ever touch the ground, ask Him to open your eyes. As your eyes open in the mornings, ask Him to open your eyes throughout the day. You will be surprised at what will come up. Also, include an opening up of your eyes to the risking crazy life that He has for you. Again, you will not know all the details, but you will be in a place of surrender. This surrender will lead your eyes to be opened to the future. You have to start with prayer.

THE BIG 3

As you start to live this life of prayer, you will need to be looking for what I call the "big 3." These are the top three priorities in your life. I do not know what they are for you; however, I trust you are far enough along in your spiritual journey that you have started to live a daily surrender to this lifestyle. If so, then you have determined what is most important in your life. This does not have to be overly complicated. For example, my "big 3" are God, wife, and kids. They are in that order. I realize that if I do not make God a priority, then I cannot live the life He is asking of me. . If I do not make my wife, Melissa, a priority, I cannot live the risking crazy lifestyle. If I do not make my kids a priority, then I have missed living the risking crazy lifestyle in my life and for future generations. My next 30 years are going to be prioritized by how I live out the risking crazy lifestyle in those three areas.

Even though God is first, this does not mean that we treat Him like a compartment in our life. He must permeate every aspect of every relationship we have. So really, God is in all and all. He must be first, middle, and last while still being at the center. Do you catch my drift? What will the next 30 years look like if at the center is God? This means in everything, He must have center stage. This is the risking crazy lifestyle.

In our culture, to put God at the center is what some might call crazy. We have reduced God down to one hour on Sunday. And to most, He is not even that. For most in our culture, He is someone we call on when we are in trouble. I might stretch it even further to say that maybe He is never called upon. If this is the case, then to live a life of risk is to put God at the center. If God is at the center for the next 30 years, how will that trickle down into your other relationships?

If you are married, your spouse needs to be in the number two spot. The truth is that your spouse cannot bring you true joy, satisfaction, and happiness. Only Jesus can do that. In many ways, when we become a follower of Jesus, we are married to Jesus. I know this sounds weird; however, the church is His bride. I think the picture of becoming one flesh is what we must focus on. As a follower of Jesus, you are one flesh with Him. We are to start becoming like Him through the power of His grace to change us. When this happens, we realize that our true joy, satisfaction, and happiness only come through Him. Therefore, it is easy then to put our spouse number two.

The significance of this number two-spot is tremendous. Remember this is the priority right under God. Sometimes in a marriage relationship the kids are number two, a career is number two, or our selfish desires are number two. When this happens, we are not living the life Jesus is calling us to. We are following what our culture tells us to do. Put yourself first. To risk crazy is to make your marriage a priority right under your relationship with Jesus. What will the next 30 years look like if you put God first and your marriage second? If we are not intentional in this marriage priority, then we will not be able to live the risking crazy lifestyle consistently.

Now I know that some reading this may be single. You might be a teenager, who has not even considered marriage yet. Or you are a young adult who is not yet married. You may not even plan on getting married. Or, maybe you're single again. Whatever the case, if you are single, you should use your singleness for Jesus. This is crazy talk in the midst of our current culture. The culture tells the single person to seek every relationship possible until you find the right one. This type of thinking and behavior will lead you to fall in and out of relationships and possibly make some major life decisions based on feelings and not the truth of God's Word. People will call you crazy. They will try to set you up on blind dates. I urge you, to pursue Jesus and allow Him to bring that spouse to you. Take this time and use it for Jesus.

Most single people have plans of getting married in the next 30 years. If this is you, setting up the best priorities first will help you decipher God's plan for you. This is why it is so vitally important for you to choose, by God's grace, your "big 3." What, according to God's Word, is important to you in a spouse? What, according to God's Word, are your top three priorities? I am going to let you figure that out. Remember, start with prayer, and allow Jesus to move your heart.

What about number three? For me, I would say that is my kids. My next 30 years, really matter. Why? Because I have kids! The number one way to impact the future is to impact your kids. I was a youth pastor. I believe in the importance of this great ministry. I believe people are called to be youth pastors; however, the youth pastor can only go so far. I remember being that guy that the parents came to expecting me to be the only spiritual influence in their kid's life. The problem with this approach is that they had more time with them than I did. I could influence their lives. I could lead them spiritually, but if it was not reinforced at home, I was teaching them something that was so counter-cultural that rarely were lives changed for the long haul.

Then there were those parents who said, "Jason, we want you to be a spiritual influence in our kid's lives; however, we understand our role is greater than yours. We promise to reinforce at home what you guide them in." When that happened, those kids ended up making long-term changes that affected other's lives for the glory of Jesus. The truth is that if you are depending on your church, youth ministry, children's ministry, or any other ministry to give your kids their only spiritual guidance, you are missing the boat. You see that is what everyone else is doing. If you want to live a lifestyle focused on what Jesus wants, you

have to make your family's spiritual welfare an intentional priority. You cannot just lease this out to the "hired professional" at
your church or Christian school. You and I as parents must take
the reins in guiding our kid's spiritual future.

If you got serious about taking risks—that some might call
crazy—by leading your family spiritually, what would the future
look like? How would those kid's lives be changed? How will
your grandkids lives be changed? As a pastor, I have seen this
happen. When we started The Vertical Church, we had "first
generation" Christians. In other words, as far as they knew, they
were the first ones in their recent family's history to become
followers of Jesus. I have literally seen entire families including grandchildren's lives changed forever because one person
became a follower and got serious about their family's spiritual
welfare.

WHAT DOES THE PREFERRED
FUTURE LOOK LIKE?

I am going to ask you in this section to really start dreaming
about the next 30 years. With the "big 3" in mind, what does that
look like? How will your relationship with Jesus change? Think
about some of the lessons learned through this book. How will
you start listening to the Spirit in every moment? If Jesus is at
the top, then things are about to change in your life. Again, we
cannot see the future. I do not want to lead you to believe that
God is about to reveal to you all the details of your future. I do
not believe that at all. In fact, I believe you have to be as general
as possible in this. One example of this might be, "In every major decision in my life, I will spend three days in prayer before
making that decision." That is just an example. I can guarantee
you there will be decisions in your life that will cause you to
pray. But before you get there, decide now how you will make

those decisions. In this new way of living, gone are the days of just trusting in your own desires. To truly risk crazy, we have to "deny ourselves."

WHAT CHANGES DO YOU NEED TO MAKE?

The book of James says this: "Do not merely listen to the word, and so deceive yourselves. Do what it says. Anyone who listens to the word but does not do what it says is like someone who looks at his face in a mirror and, after looking at himself, goes away and immediately forgets what he looks like. But whoever looks intently into the perfect law that gives freedom, and continues in it—not forgetting what they have heard, but doing it—they will be blessed in what they do" (James 1:22-25).

I have heard it said that some scholars in the past wanted to rip the book of James out of the Bible because of the "works emphasis." But I have to disagree. If we take the entire Bible as a whole, we will see that we can do these works because of the great grace that Jesus has given us.

The reason we should choose to live the lifestyle faith risks is the risk that Jesus took on us. When we start to fathom the amount of mercy and grace that He gave us, we will be spurred on to do good works. This a foundation of grace is what urges us to live the Word of God in our life. It is through this grace that we now can live lives of risk.

The bottom line is that you have to decide to make some changes. As you look 30 years ahead and gather your "big 3" priorities, you will have to make daily changes as you deny yourself, take up your cross, and follow Him. He will call you to change. You will read and hear the Word and then must become doers of that Word. If not, then it is all in vain. You have not truly understood the greatness of the grace that was afforded you in your salvation. The only outcome of a life touched by grace is change.

Let me illustrate this for you. If you were to say that your number two priority in the next 30 years is your marriage, what changes might Jesus be calling you to make. Maybe your priority sentence you write is something like this: "I want to still be married to my spouse in 30 years while growing in friendship and intimacy." It is vague yet specific in values. If you have a statement like this, you will need to be intentional about changing the way you view your spouse. You will need to start looking at them through the eyes of Jesus. So something you might start making a practice of is daily asking Jesus to help you see them as He sees them. If you did this every day for 30 years, do you think you would meet the priority stated in that sentence? Absolutely. When we ask, He listens, and answers.

It is time to start allowing the Spirit to make the changes in your life that correlate to taking risks for Jesus. Notice the last part of what James says, "...not forgetting what they have heard, but doing it—they will be blessed." Will you actually change and do what God is asking you to do? Whose life will be different? How will the next 30 years be different? What life will be changed for eternity? Your kindness, your ability, your sheer knowledge of the Word says one thing: Be the change! Without the people in the church being the church, we have lost our impact. The Spirit that raised Jesus from the dead lives inside of us and gives us the ability and power to carry out anything He asks of us. Will you take the challenge and live the risking crazy lifestyle?

WHAT WILL YOUR LEGACY BE?

Imagine with me. You are at the end of your life. You have lived a long life, but now it has come to an end. You stand before

God. Because of your faith in Jesus, He says, "Enter in." Before you enter, He stops you and says, "I want to show you something." Of course, you say, "Ok." I mean who is going to turn down God showing them something. At that moment a screen of your life appears. It is you sitting in your church. You are dressed nice with your family beside you. You nod in agreement with the sermon and sing praise to Him through your song. But at that moment before the service ends, you see what you now remember. It is that moment when the God of the universe nudges you and asks you to step out in faith and risk crazy. He asks you to believe. You now see that thought process played out before your very eyes.

Your mind goes through all the excuses.

"I can't do that."

"Maybe that was just something I ate."

"Really God? Me?"

"What time is the football game today?"

"I would fail at that."

Excuse after excuse comes in your mind, now on display in front of you and the God of the universe. As each excuse passes, the voice of God that day starts to get softer and softer, quieter and quieter until it fades away with your mind shifting gears to think about the after service festivities for the day.

At that moment, you are thinking. "I'm glad that is over." As soon as that scene ends another day pops up. This time you are sitting at your favorite Starbucks. As you ponder the day, you look out the window and there sits that same homeless person you see every time you go in. Something pricks your heart. For some reason this time a thought pops in your mind, "Buy that man a drink and some food." Again, while standing before God, the excuses are played out on the screen of your life:

"I'm in a hurry."

"What if he robs me?"

"What will one drink and muffin do?"

"He needs a job."

"Was that the voice of God?"

Again, excuse after excuse plays out. Yes, it might be a risk that some will call crazy. The voice of God then becomes an afterthought.

At that moment, God raises His hand as if to stop the video from rolling. He then looks at you and says, "All those times, I was speaking to you. I was asking you to deny yourself, take up your cross, and follow me. I did not give you all the details because I wanted you to trust Me. I really wish you would have trusted me. You see I was calling you in that moment to change the world. Yes, it was a small part, but it was your part. What could have happened through you would have changed your life. I am sorry you did not take me up on those offers."

As you stand there speechless, you realize that you missed many opportunities. Truthfully that scenario will probably not play out in heaven, but we miss out on opportunities every day. God is asking you to stop today and tomorrow and obey that simple, small, still voice to risk crazy for Him.

Do not get me wrong. God is sovereign. With or without you, He will accomplish His will. But don't you want to be included in it? Don't you want to see what God has for you? Don't you want to play your part in helping bring change to this world for His glory?

I do. I have settled in my heart that I will do what it takes to obey as much as I can those promptings. I do not claim to be perfect in this. I will make many mistakes. I will not obey at times. This is why I am thankful for grace. But at the same time, I do not want to miss out on any opportunity that He has for me for His glory. Why not live life to make Jesus famous? Why not make this our legacy?

In everything, above everything, let us make Jesus the centerpiece. I do not want to stand before God and say, "God, I attended church every Sunday. I read my Bible. I went to Sunday School. I even said 'Amen' a few times to the sermon." Is this all we have reduced this following Jesus to? I believe that following Him is much more than going to a building once or three times a week. It is about waking up to the voice of the Spirit in you in every moment carrying out the small promptings to risk crazy. If we lived with this in mind, we could make a bigger impact than we currently do.

What will be your legacy? Will it be all about Jesus? There is only one way to make that happen. You have to decide today that you will live the risking crazy lifestyle. You have to decide tomorrow to do it again. Then a year from now, when it gets tough and the enemy is fighting tooth and nail to tear you down, you have to surrender again. We cannot give up. Ever. We cannot allow our selfish desires to drive us. We cannot allow our comfort to drive us. We cannot allow our insecurities to drive us. We must rise above.

If our legacy counts, then why not make it count for something that will last for an eternity. That something is someone. His name is Jesus. He is calling you today to take risks—that some might call crazy—for Him. So go ahead, pull that cord, and hang on for the ride of your life!

NEXT STEPS

1. Set aside some time to spend with God in prayer asking Him to open your mind about your next 30 years.
2. If you were to dream 30 years ahead, what would the "big 3" priorities of your life be?
3. As you rank your priorities, write one-sentence dreams about each one of them.

4. Based on God's Word, what changes will you need to make in the next month to start accomplishing the dreams for the "big 3"?

5. How will you take what you have learned in this book and live it out on a daily basis?

6. In one sentence, write down what you want your legacy to be.

Visit the author at www.jasontayloruma.com.

CPSIA information can be obtained at www.ICGtesting.com
Printed in the USA
LVOW07s0821151015

458353LV00004B/7/P